MAKE MONEY WITH

SHOPIFY

FOR BEGINNERS

Your easy guide to passive recurring
online income, you have our instead

BAXTER TOMS

Make money with Shopify for beginners

Your easy guide to passive recurring online income

by Baxter Toms

Passive Recurring Income with Shopify

Table of Contents

Chapter 1

Introduction to Shopify andPassive Recurring Income

Making a living as a blogger is a dream shared by many – and it's easy to see why it has such appeal. As a full time blogger, you can make a full time living writing about any subject in the word, which will normally mean you're writing about something you love and find fascinating.

At the same time, blogging means you can potentially earn a living from anywhere in the world. You could be earning money while sitting on a sunny beach, or while travelling the globe!

Then there's the fact that bloggers get to enjoy a semblance of fame. In their niche/industry, bloggers will be well recognized and will have fans and followers who hang off of their every word – that's a great feeling.

Let's not forget that blogging can make you a *nice* amount of money!

So you're earning a lot of money, you're not having to worry about a boss and you're doing all that from wherever you want in the world. You're writing a subject you love and you'll have a roster of fans around the globe who hang off of your every word.

So is this the perfect business model?

Not quite. Unfortunately, monetizing a traditional website or blog can be tricky. After all, you're giving away the main bulk of everything you create completely for free! The whole idea of a blog is that you're adding content where anyone can find it and so why would anyone need to pay you?

This means you then need to either sell a product from your site and use your content to promote that product, or you need to use advertising and rely on lots of people visiting your site and clicking your ads.

Can this work? Sure! There are plenty of people on the web who make millions from these kinds of business models.

But unfortunately, it's also a lot of work and very unstable.

Getting your number of unique daily hits to the point where you can make a solid income from a regular website or blog is going to be tough for starters. This will take a considerable amount of SEO, social media marketing and most important of all – luck.

And then, at any moment, everything you've built for yourself could come crashing down. It only takes for Google to change its algorithm, for Facebook to change their policies or for your competition to release a better product and your income can be effectively cut off at source overnight.

The life of a blogger or a website owner then is a rather difficult one without any stable form of income and with no guarantee that money will be coming in from one month to the next.

Getting a home loan can be an absolute nightmare!

And this is where Shopify comes in. Shopify and recurring passive income.

Welcome to the best-kept secret in internet marketing. Membership sites are *the* way to monetize your efforts online and as you'll see – they can solve all of the problems that we just described.

What is Passive Recurring Income?
In this book, we're going to look at some of the different ways you can earn money from your site using Shopify. You'll do this by creating a membership site but also by selling subscriptions to other things – things like email courses and discount memberships.

And all these methods are going to allow you to set up what's known as 'passive recurring income'. What does this mean though?

Well, you know what income means. It means money! So this is a revenue stream that will ensure you have a steady flow of cash coming into your account.

How about the other two words?

Passive means that the income carries on coming in even when you're not doing any work. You could be asleep or sitting on that aforementioned sunny beach and you'll still have cash flowing in all the while. Imagine being able to go on holiday with your friends and knowing that you're still earning money every minute you're out there... It's great!

No longer are you trading your time for cash. No longer do you need to be in a constant rush – this buys you the kind of freedom that you can only imagine.

Now what about recurring?

Well this is the part that makes a membership site very different from any other kind of blog. This is the bit that gives you as steady income that isn't reliant on everything going smoothly. This is where you get the *guarantee*.

Recurring income simply means that you're going to have a payment system set up, so that your customers/clients/fans are paying you on a weekly, monthly or quarterly basis and you can therefore predict exactly how much money you're going to make.

Suddenly, that unpredictability is gone. Suddenly, it's much easier to get that home loan. Now you can start planning for the long term based on how much money you *know* you have coming in next month.

Chapter 2

How to Make Recurring Incomewith Shopify

So traditional blogging isn't the perfect business model but this just might be. By setting up recurring passive income, you'll be earning guaranteed and predictable cash, while you sleep.

How's that possible?

Simple: by using Shopify and building a membership site or subscription product.

What is Shopify?

Shopify is basically an ecommerce solution. This makes it very similar to something like Magento or WooCommerce.

Ecommerce simply means that you're creating an online store – like Amazon – where people can buy products from the comfort of your home, thereby earning you cash.

Shopify differentiates itself from other ecommerce platforms in a number of ways though. For starters, Shopify is *hosted*. That means that you don't need to install it yourself on your own server – instead you just sign up and create your own account and store just as you would if you were on a social network like Facebook.

And because Shopify is hosted, this means it's rather powerful. While some self-hosted options severely limit the number of items you can have in stock, Shopify lets you sell up to 5,000 items from your store at once.

Shopify is exceedingly quick and simple to get started with, so if you want to add any kind of ecommerce to your site and start selling ebooks, courses or physical products... well then this is a great way to start out. In fact, it only takes a few clicks to get set up with your own store!

There are many more cool features that Shopify offers. One particularly neat one is the option to use your own POS – Point Of Sale device – in the real world. So if you had a physical highstreet store *and* an online store, you could sync up your inventory and take orders on the go using a chip and pin device. Imagine being able to head out into the street and sell your ebooks to passers-by!

You can try it out with a free 14-day trial too, so it's worth giving it a go.

Getting Started

To get started, click on 'Start Your Free Trial' and then just enter your email address, password and a name for your store.

On the next page, you'll be given the option to add your details such as your location and your phone number. This is for tax purposes so that the store knows how to handle the legal side of things.

The next page says 'Tell us a little about yourself'. Here you just need to answer a couple of questions such as whether you're already selling products, how much your business is making and whether you're developing for yourself or for a client.

Once you've done that, you'll be in! From here you can see some of the different options for your store which will include the option to access settings (where you can change things like the name of your store) and where you can start adding items and creating your store.

To start creating your store, click '**Add Online Store**'. You can then choose a theme for your store. There are plenty of themes that are available complete for free and these will be easy to install with the click of a button and then to customize.

If you want to get a little more professional and fancy with your store, then you can go to the Theme Store to select from numerous other free and premium themes. Click 'customize theme' to edit what your store looks like and change things like the logo, the heading and the arrangement of items on the page when people first load up. Once you're happy, hit '**Publish Theme**' and you're ready to go!

On the next tab, you have the option to select 'Navigation' which will let you add individual pages and content. This is where you'll put your 'About Us' information, a blog etc.

You can use 'set up a custom domain' to use your current web address (www.example.com/shop) and to add your first product you simply have to click '**Add a Product**' from the front page.

To add products, you're just going to enter a title, an image and set a few elements like the price. With a little more setting up (you'll need to add your own details to get paid for instance) this is how quickly and simply you can start selling products!

Adding Apps
On its own, Shopify is a very powerful tool with a lot of great features for creating your online store. However, in order to set up our online business with passive recurring income, we're going to need some even more powerful and tailored features.

Fortunately, Shopify has essentially limitless capability thanks to the existence of an app store. For those familiar with WordPress (which you hopefully will be), this section of Shopify works very much like the plugins section of WordPress and extends the capabilities of your store.

Some apps are premium and will require you to pay extra for their use. Others however are completely free – particularly those that are provided by Shopify itself.

In order to start looking for apps, use the burger menu on the left hand side of the screen and select (you guessed it) 'apps'.

From here, you can then search for apps and you'll be able to see the price and ratings alongside each listing. Once you find the one you want, click to install and then confirm.

To start with, try adding the '**Digital Downloads**' app.

This is a basic and free app that essentially gives you the ability to sell digital products like ebooks and apps from your store and have them delivered automatically. This way, you don't need to send out an email with an attachment each time an order comes through and you can just let Shopify handle that for you.

This is pretty handy seeing as we're trying to generate *passive* income here – you don't want your sunny beach holiday to be ruined by hundreds of emails with product purchases! At the same time, this will ensure that your buyers get their products *instantly* rather than having to wait for you to send the email if you're asleep. This is particularly important if you intend on selling to an international audience.

Click to install this app and then find your product listing. On the page where you're selling your product, click the button at the top with the three dots and this will open up a list of actions that are made possible by the apps you have installed. You should now see the option to 'add digital attachment' and once you click this, you'll be taken to a page where you can add your file. Nice and easy! From now on, when someone buys that product, they'll be sent an email with the file attached and they can enjoy it without you having to lift a finger.

That's service!

This was just an example though. If you're building a subscription service you might want to hang on for a moment as we'll be looking at another option for your digital downloads.

Have a look through the apps because you'll find there are all kinds of useful things you can use here to add to your store. One great one is a '**Preorder Manager**' which will allow you to set up pre-orders for your products. The possibilities here are huge – you can generate a lot of buzz for a product and then collect funds ready to launch. You could even run your own crowd funding campaign without having to hand any of your hard-earned funds over to Kick starter!

Chapter 3

Apps to Use to Collect Recurring Payments

Okay, now we're getting close to setting up our first membership site or subscription service. You're so close you can smell it I bet!

As you might have guessed, setting up subscriptions and recurring payments will require the use of another app. There are actually several you can use here. **Recurring Orders** by "boldapps" is one option. Others include **Chargebee**, **Recurring Billing**, **Subscription Order** and **Charge Rabbit**.

Most of these options will cost you around $20 a month to use– so you need to work this into your calculations when deciding whether it's worth it for you or not.

One of the options that's free though at the time of writing is Charge Rabbit (https://apps.shopify.com/charge-rabbit). A neat feature for this one is integration with another app called 'Sky Pilot' which is another digital downloads plugin. The great thing about combining these two then, is that you can sell a monthly membership that will deliver PDFs, videos or any other kind of file each month. This is a perfect way to set up a business selling PDFs or

Of course you do get what you pay for to some extent and you can expect that paying a little more will get you more features. At the end of the day, it's up to you whether you want to pay a little more or whether you're happy with a more basic service.

With Charge Rabbit installed, you'll then need to set up a Stripe account, choose your payment system and then setup customer accounts within your Shopify store. Stripe is a tool that allows you to charge people in much the same way as PayPal. If you would rather use PayPal to collect your payments, then you might want to use another plugin.

This is the basic system you'll use for most of the plugins and apps. Creating a profile for each member is of course important so that you can track who has paid and who hasn't and help them to receive their products automatically.

If you are selling a subscription to your website, then you'll need to create a 'members only' area. You can do this by again using a number of plugins. Most of these plugins will require you to set up and create accounts for your individual paying customers when they pay for your products.

Chapter 4

Types of Products To Sell on Subscriptions for Recurring Income

Okay, so now you have your Shopify Store and you know how to add apps to charge recurring payments, the next step is to start actually adding those products so that you have something to sell.

This is going to work just the same as adding *any* kind of product to an ecommerce store. The only difference is that the product is going to need to be the kind of thing that people are willing to pay a recurring fee for.

This is where things get a little tricky. If you're selling an ebook from your site currently for instance, then that's just not going to work – people only want to pay for ebooks once and from there they expect to get as much access as they could possibly want!

The point is that different types of product work different for different types of business model. For subscription sites, you need a *very* specific type of product that people will be happy to pay for regularly and that they will be happy to make such a commitment to.

Let's take a look at some of the types of products that work particularly well for this model...

Subscription Sites

The title of this ebook is 'Shopify Membership Sites', so perhaps that's the best place to start. A membership site is of course a website that you charge people to become a member of and by doing this, you'll thereby grant them additional access to more materials on your site.

To make this work, you need to understand why someone would be moved to sign up to a membership site in the first place. The answer is because you offer great value on a recurring basis and they don't want to miss everything that you'll be uploading.

At the same time though, there's also something psychological going on here: people like to be 'members' of things because it makes them feel like part of a community or movement and because it makes them feel important.

If you want to help your membership site thrive then, you need to offer the kind of content that people can't get anywhere else, you need to make that content comprehensive and you need to create an excitement and buzz around your community. On the public areas of your site, tease people by saying how your 'VIP members' have access to exclusive information and share the kinds of exciting and valuable discussions that are going on in your forums.

On your site, you might want to consider adding the following things to make membership all the more enticing:

- A members' forum – If you can build a big community around your site then this will be a huge boon in general and will keep people coming back. If you then have a restricted area where the really exciting discussion happens, a lot of people will be willing to take the leap.
- Premium content – What counts as premium content? This will be just like the free content on your site (which you still need to provide to keep your visitors biting) but it will probably be a lot more comprehensive, in-depth and well put-together. Better yet, try to make sure that your premium content delivers some kind of value that will provide a real 'takeaway' for your readers. Solve a problem, or help them with their own business so that they can see ROI from signing up. That latter option is a *very* reliable way to get more subscribers and to keep your existing members happy.
- Index/Repository – If you can create some kind of comprehensive resource on your website, then this is a fantastic thing you can charge membership for. Create the definitive index of information, tools and more on your website and make sure that it offers *real* value to your users so they keep opening it.

Newsletters and Ezines

Using the combination of Sky Pilot and Charge Rabbit, we've seen that it's very easy to charge a recurring fee for digital products that you deliver each month.

So what kind of product would work well here?

There are plenty of different options but a particularly good one is to send out a weekly or monthly newsletter or ezine. Of course this will need to offer more value than your typical 'free' newsletter, so make sure you're providing real value. One great example of how you can do this is by updating your readers with insider industry news that helps them with their own businesses.

Courses

Another popular type of subscription service utilizing digital products is a course. Send weekly or monthly emails and you can train your customers to learn a variety of skills or to set up their own business. Instead of selling an ebook for a one off price, why not split those chapters into individual lessons and send them out on a monthly basis? You can actually charge more this way and at the same time it will *feel* like less of an investment for your customers. Video course also work very well.

Web Apps

A web app can be anything from a business tool to an entertainment tool. Feedly, Evernote and Netflix are all examples of subscription-apps that have a paid option. If you are handy with code and you have a good idea, this is a great way to offer value and to charge a recurring fee for it.

Physical Products

Believe it or not, a subscription model can also help you to sell physical products. This will only be suitable for certain businesses but there are some great examples of subscription-based-serves online at the moment.

One of the best of these examples is the subscription diet service that sends you food that will be tasty, save time and help them lose weight/eat more healthily. You can even get clothes on subscription that send out a selection of clothes items that will look stylish and fit you – these are great because they prevent your wardrobe from stagnating.

Use a bit of imagination – nearly any product you sell can be turned into a subscription service. Now you have the means, think about how you can provide something better for your customers *and* better for your bottom line!

Chapter 5

How to Promote Your Shopify Subscription Site - Tips and Tricks to Get More Paying Members

Okay, now you have your store, the next trick is to start getting some actual customers!

To this end, there are a number of different internet marketing techniques you can use and largely this will be the same as marketing any other kind of blog or ecommerce store. At the same time though, there are also some additional methods you can employ to help convert your visitors into happy subscribers.

Internet Marketing for Ecommerce

As far as internet marketing goes, all the usual strategies apply.

The most important of these is going to be content marketing. Just to bring you up to speed, content marketing essentially means creating a blog and then adding lots of great content to it. This works wonders because it means that you give your visitors a reason to keep coming back – so that they can read more and more of what you're uploading.

At the same time though, content marketing is also crucial for SEO (search engine optimization) because content is what Google is looking for on your website. Additionally, content helps your social media marketing because it's what people are going to share on social media.

Content marketing becomes even more crucial if you are selling membership to a website because this is what will serve as your free 'sample' of what visitors will eventually be paying for. Make sure to add content regularly then to either an external blog or the blog page on your Shopify store and at the same time, be sure to include subtle use of keywords so that your content shows up on Google.

Another useful tool is PPC. PPC is 'Pay Per Click' advertising and is one of the main forms of advertising online. Look into Google AdWords and Facebook Ads and use these to get paid exposure for your site.

A mailing list is another very useful tool that you can use to build trust over time and then convert readers into buyers!

How to Get More Subscribers

Here are just a few tricks you can use to get more subscribers:

- Offer a 'free trial' of some sort – If your product is genuinely good, then this is a great way to get people hooked
- Offer discounts – A short-term discount is a great way to create urgency and to get more clicks
- Use your existing members – A strategy many subscription sites use is to offer discounts to members who manage to bring in more members. This is a set-up that benefits everyone!

Chapter 6

Other Tools for Shopify

The great thing about Shopify is just how packed with apps and features it is. There are so many here that you can create whole new business models and marketing opportunities just by clicking and installing a couple. Here are some that are worth checking out.

Chimpified

Chimpified is a great app for anyone who has a MailChimp account. MailChimp is of course an autoresponder that lets you create a mailing list. By using Chimpified though, you can integrate this with your Shopify account and thereby use cookies in order to identify the behaviour of your subscribers. For example, you can use remarketing and send targeted emails to your visitors based on what products they looked at!

Plugin SEO

This helps to automate a lot of the complicated SEO stuff for your store – now you can get more visitors from Google without having to worry about things like meta tags!

Shopify Widgets

If you have a website already, this will let you add products and services to your site in the sidebar. This is a great way to get more exposure and it also means you can embed your stock elsewhere!

LeadDyno

Why would someone else want to feature your products? Why, if you were to sell affiliate products of course! This way you can share commission with other marketers and have a legion of people promoting your items!

ShopPad

This is a useful plugin that will let you take your Shopify store and turn it into an iPad/Android friendly store. The store is well optimized for mobile anyway but this will make it even easier for mobile users.

Mobile App for Your Shop by Shoutem

Better yet, why not create an actual app version of your store!

Facebook Store

This is an incredibly powerful plugin that can turn your Facebook page into a Shopify store. In other words, anyone who likes your page will now have the option to buy your products and even sign up for a subscription *through* that page. This is a fantastic way to fully monetize your Facebook marketing efforts.

Chapter 7

Other Ways to Provide Subscriptions with Physical and Digital Products

At this point you're probably in no doubt as to the potential power of a subscription site or product. With a subscription you can sell recurring memberships and charge your customers on a regular basis and that way finally have some kind of stability and predictability in your online business model. This makes a *huge* difference and of course there's no reason you can use both recurring subscription products *and* your current advertising/one off sales revenue at the same time.

But perhaps this all seems like an awful lot of work? Maybe you're feeling anxious about the idea of creating an ecommerce store? Or perhaps you don't have a big enough audience, a website or any content.

In these cases, there are some alternative options you can use.

One such option is to use **Ecom Subscription Pro**

This is a product that will give you a ready-made sales funnel, products and an ecommerce solution all in one package. In other words, this is all the work done for you – a ready-made subscription-based business that you can simply download, set-up and start profiting from on a recurring basis. This is an incredibly simple way to start earning recurring payments and to live the dream of truly passive, recurring income!

Another option is YouTube. YouTube now lets creators set up paid content on YouTube (https://support.google.com/youtube/answer/3249127?hl=en) which can also include subscription offers (https://support.google.com/youtube/answer/3249131). If you have a website but you don't want to worry about setting up an online store, installing plugins or dealing with sales funnels – then having a subscription channel on YouTube is a great way around this. You can charge as much as you like and as long as you put in some work to create high quality videos, there's no reason you can't turnover a *large* amount of cash on a regular and reliable basis.

Don't have the know-how to create your own YouTube content that people would be happy to pay for? There are a number of ways you can get around this limitation. One is of course to pay someone to create content for you. As long as you can get enough subscribers, then you can turnover a nice profit this way!

Another option is to think of some of the other ways you can create video content. You don't need to have the directorial abilities of Steven Spielberg or the presentation skills of Steve Jobs to have your own successful video content. In fact, you don't even need a camera! Did you know you can create PowerPoint presentations and then simply export those as MPGs? This way you can create tutorials, educational videos and more. Other options include using screen captures or doodle animations. Either way, this can be a great way to sell subscription content without the hassle – if you can find viewers on YouTube then you won't even necessarily need a website or any other platform of your own.

Finally, a third option is to use a WordPress *only* subscription service for your website. If your main aim is to charge for restricted content on your website, then the best method might be to use a plugin such as s2Member (http://wordpress.org/plugins/s2member/) which will allow you to charge subscribers by PayPal while bypassing the need for an ecommerce store like Shopify. Best of all, s2Member is free and it allows up to four 'levels' of membership. The plugin has very good ratings and a lot of downloads, so give it a look!

Chapter 9
Conclusion

And there you have it – a ton of options to help you get set up with recurring income using either Shopify or one of a number of other methods.

Hopefully you now recognize the huge potential for setting up recurring payments and how this can transform your business and your profits. If you have been consistently delivering value to your customers and you've built up trust over the years, then you'll be surprised just how willing they are to pay for more content and services from you.

At the same time, subscription payments can work wonders for selling digital *or* physical products and can even help you to provide an even better service. Get creative and look for ways to sell your products as subscriptions and you can drastically increase your revenue and your customer loyalty.

Your Shopify cheat sheet

Your Shopify Membership Site Cheat Sheet

If you've read the full ebook by now, then hopefully you should be brimming with ideas and inspiration for your own membership services and ecommerce stores. There are tons of ways you can utilize these elements to create novel business models and any of these methods will lead to a reliable and stable monthly income.

Keep this cheat sheet nearby as you execute your plan and it will walk you through the process of getting set up with your store from start to finish.

The Steps

1. Create a website or blog. The best way to do this is by creating a WordPress site which is very simple and easy.
2. Set up your Shopify account – just register by entering your details.
3. Create your store – this involves choosing a theme and customizing a few elements to suit your niche.
    a. Adding a logo can be a useful way to increase brand awareness
4. If you want to add any basic products then just click to add your product
    a. Choose some images
    b. Set a price
    c. Write a short description
5. Many marketers reading this will be selling predominantly digital products such as ebooks and apps. To sell these you'll want to add a 'digital delivery' app such as 'Sky Pilot'.
    a. This will require a Stripe account
    b. If you'd rather accept payments by PayPal, then consider using a different plugin
6. In order to accept monthly or otherwise recurring payments, you'll also want to install another app. One of the best options is Charge Rabbit – because it's free and it integrates seamlessly with Sky Pilot.
7. Create your subscription product
    a. If you want to make your website a membership site, then you'll need to create a 'members' area' for your site and/or the store itself
8. Promote your store!

Types of Subscription Product

There are many types of subscription product that you can sell from your website, with some working better than others.

In order to charge a recurring fee, it is generally necessary for your product to offer recurring value. This needs to be something that people look at/use regularly.

Options include:

- A newsletter or ezine – Make sure this has high production values and that you are offering some kind of measurable value. A good way to do the latter is to write an industry newsletter for instance and to update visitors with the very latest news and tips – this way they can see your product as helping them to increase their ROI. High quality video and images will add further value.
- Forum membership – If you can create a community that discusses information that can't be found anywhere else, then you can again charge a lot for membership. Communities are great at promoting themselves too and this can create some very loyal customers/fans. Especially if they make friends through your site!
- Physical products – Numerous physical products can work well for subscription sales techniques. Some examples of how to use this kind of business model for a physical product include:
  - o Selling disposables – Things like face creams or protein shakes run out and so may require regular restocking.
  - o Bundles and packages – Selling ingredients to cook diet friendly meals, or clothes to create new outfits are both tried and tested means of selling products on a subscription basis. You can even sell a mystery packs.
  - o Gifts – Gifts work well as a recurring purchase too. For instance a customer might want to send flowers every year on a friends' birthday!
- Courses/Lessons – Lessons and courses lend themselves very well to being delivered in instalments.
- Stories/Entertainment – You can sell a subscription to web episodes or comic strips if you are creatively minded!

Useful Apps and Tools

Some of the best apps and tools for Shopify include:

Chimpified – For integrating your mailing list with your Shopify store. You should be able to find similar tools for Aweber and the like.

Plugin SEO – This will automatically handle SEO for your store.

Shopify Widgets – Add widgets with your products to any website.

LeadDyno – Offer affiliate programs to get more people selling your products on your behalf!

Mobile App for Your Shop – Turn your Shopify store into an app

Facebook Store – Add your Shopify store to your Facebook page and let visitors buy through it directly

This is only short sample of the available tools and apps. All of these are available from the app store but be sure to look for more!

More Ways to Charge Subscription Fees

Email Subscription Pro
https://ecomsubscriptionpr
o.com

This is a 'plug and play' subscription service that doesn't use Shopify. You get an entire sales funnel and lots more here to automatically start profiting from a recurring business model.

YouTube
https://support.google.com/youtube/answer/32491
27?hl=en

YouTube now allows its creators to charge for their content. And among the various options is the ability to charge a subscription fee to see all the latest videos. If you know how to create video content and especially if you already have a popular channel, then this can be a great way to monetize!

WordPress
http://wordpress.org/plugins/s2me
mber/

Using this plugin you can charge a subscription fee for membership to your WordPress site. There's no need to create a Shopify store and you can use PayPal to accept payments which is very handy. This is one of the quicker and easier ways to add a subscription element to your current business model.

Remember there are also a number of other ecommerce stores, most of which provide similar options and plugins. Some of the most popular alternatives are Magento, WooCommerce and Volusion. Research the differences and decide which one is best for you.

And there you have it: all the tools, tips and steps you need to create your subscription business model and to start profiting. There are tons of options here and the huge range of apps available for Shopify mean you'll never run out of ideas or options.

As long as you keep providing value, you'll keep growing your list of subscribers!

Be successful online!

Making Success A Daily Part of Your Online Business Life

In this short but powerful section we are going to go over things that you can do to increase your daily success in your online business.

Your success in your online business can be achieved in many different ways. One of the biggest things that keep small business owners from staying successful is the ability to stay focused and stay motivated in their business.

Over the pages that follow were going to discuss different ways that you can stay motivated and focused so you can maximize every possible opportunity that comes your way.

Even in today's economy opportunity is all around us you just have to reach out and take advantage of all of the opportunities that are available to you if you wish to seize all the success that is available to you and your business.

So that said let's get started so that by this time next week you can Own Your Online Success.

What We Will Cover

✓ To demonstrate that to move forward, if you haven't been doing so recently, something needs to change.

✓ To show you that no matter how idealistic it sounds, opportunity is everywhere.

✓ To display the need to understand such concepts if being a success at anything is something you want to be.

✓ To lay the groundwork and introduce the concept of business contacts for future reports.

✓ To show you that scientifically, the possibilities of achieving whatever you want is possible through business contacts and to demonstrate this process happening as we speak.

✓ To help explain exactly how you are in complete control of your situation, now and into the future.

✓ To display how your situation can change in an instant, and how you're about to make that happen for yourself.

✓ To get you up off the chair and creating opportunity for yourself with the knowledge that it will move your forward towards your goals quickly and effectively.

✓ To overcome the fear of not being able to move forward, or being too far away from your goals, making the job to reach them look huge, when really, it's nothing more than a few steps away.

Opportunity Is Everywhere

Let me start off by saying that this is report is totally unplanned, it's coming straight from inside my head, and for good reason. My aim here is to let you know a little bit about my personal thoughts relating to opportunity, how I know that this is fact, how it presents itself to you, how to spot it, and most importantly, how it relates to online marketing and you as a success. This is not a step-by-step how to, but it's been as important as ever in getting me to where I am now, and it's likely that it'll do the same for you if you can keep an open mind.

I'll be honest, I'm not really a big fan of the whole idea of positive thinking will get you where you want to be and that kind of stuff. My train of thought is more that 'it's not what you know, but who you know'. Delving into a little bit of reasoning before we get started, let me ask you a quick question. Have you ever woken up one day and realized that you totally missed a great opportunity the night before? Maybe it was a promotion, an opportunity to meet someone really interesting, or failed to take part in an activity that you wish you would have taken part in?

How about a more long-term view? Let's say you dwell on something that's happened in the past that you wish you'd done differently, or someone you wish you'd met when you had the chance, or anything relating to missed opportunities.

I'm pretty sure we've all done that, myself included, but have you ever pondered where you might be if you'd just gone for it and taken up the offer, or gone ahead with your idea? This is something that I like to look out for in the online business world and turn it on its head, instead, looking at the present. All day, every day new opportunities present themselves, and I think it's really important that an online marketer can understand when, where and how this happens, and how to take advantage of it, which we can't do without first being able to spot the potential that arises from particular situations.

Now, I'm big on making contacts and creating mutual business partnerships with other marketers that benefit both parties. However, I rarely see anyone actually make this effort consistently and on a long term basis, which is a shame, because we'd all have exactly what we wanted already if we helped each other out a little more.

Let me explain. I read about a scientific study of sorts (that you may or may not be familiar with) that suggests every single person in the world, no matter where they are, what country they're in or what language they speak, is connected and knows you through a chain of seven people. They took this random hermit type guy that lives a very solitary life in the mountains of a far off country, and picked out a person in the London area to test this.

Through research and a little bit of juggling here and there, they managed to get from this person in London, to the other person living in the mountains in a far off country with his animals in seven jumps, a friend of a friend of a friend and so on. My first point here is a very important one. Whether this theory is dead accurate or not, opportunities are indeed out there, and you should take a little bit of time out to see this, and you'll immediately notice that they aren't as far away as you might think, no matter how desperate the situation.

Let's imagine for a moment, you're an online marketer with a modest business, earning a couple of thousand dollars a month. How long will it take you to hit the big time? Who knows, the big contacts and deals that could catapult you right up there through mutual agreement and benefit could be just one or two conversations away. Your new business partner could be waiting for you just around the corner and you could meet at any time.

My Biggest Tip

This is my first point to every single online marketer out there. If I had five minutes to talk to every single person with an online business, looking for advice, this is what I'd tell them. Opportunities exist, all kinds of opportunities, things that might not have even been thought about. They're everywhere and if you want to be a great success, they need to be taken advantage of at every step.

Don't get me wrong, I'm not saying you'll wake up tomorrow with an e-mail in your inbox that'll answer all your problems, but seriously, solutions and new partnerships are out there ripe for the taking, which brings me on to the next point. If you don't take them, someone else will. Don't wait for them to come to you, get out there and dig them up.

This is how the big guys out there make things happen. They don't do things alone, they make their contacts, and they assist each other, whether it be an intentional, or purely circumstantial meeting, a big group of people are making sure each other is successful. Let's take just ten marketers for example. Each one has ten times more promotion power, ten times the chance of meeting new contacts to increase their chances further, ten times the income, and so on. You have to be able to see the power of this.

Look at it this way. Imagine the room you're sitting in is painted pure white from top to bottom, floors and all. Now take a thin nib pen, and draw a small black dot on your wall. This is you. Now take a red pen and place a small dot above yourself for each one of your friends, then a blue pen for each one of your friends, friends.

Imagine this process repeating itself again and again, until your wall is full. See all those dots? Each one is an opportunity, each one a different person from a different walk of life that you have a chance to meet, learn from and become mutual successes. Whether they just give you a new perspective on things, or whether they give you a small helpful tip, or become your long term business partner, whatever it is, it's there, it's closer than you think and it's waiting for someone to pick up and take it to the next level, and at the same time become a success. If that's not you, it'll be someone else.

Taking Success

To each one of these people you have something to offer, as they no doubt have something to offer to you. Don't get me wrong, I'm not suggesting that you should go out and make friends with the whole of the world's population, but I really want to make it clear how these opportunities are there, and they're ready for you to take them in whatever form you wish.

This is the most important thing that I believe I can show you. If you see something you like, don't sit back and say Ah that's pretty cool, jump up and grab it with both hands. It's yours to take right now. Don't hesitate.

One more small analogy and I'll tell you a little story about how this very site came to be, and most likely many other sites and businesses before and after it. Imagine you're walking down an isle in a crowded shopping mall. Who was that person you just brushed arms with? Was it the guy that's going to tell his friends about your business and what you do, leading to five new customers? Is this the woman that's going to give you a free beauty consultation in the future? Is it the guy that's going to tell his friend about your business, and hook you up with a massive marketing campaign to their list?

The potential here is totally massive. Hold up though, there's something very important that you should know about this connection making process, and that's that it's give and take. In a business sense, it's likely you'll be giving them something and they'll be giving you something valuable in return.

This type of business has been around for so long now. All we're looking at is trades that are mutually beneficial to each party. One thing I would like to say before we go any further here, is that I'm talking in a purely business sense. I don't seriously look at everyone I meet as a new money making machine, and I don't advise anyone do that either. All I'm suggesting here, with these rather black and white examples, is that the opportunity is out there if you're willing to take it and the results can be huge.

We'll be talking a little later about how to make contacts, and actual methods of doing so, simply because I believe that it's the path to total success in whatever you're trying to do. Even if it seems like you're getting a pay cut of sorts in the short term. Stop trying to do things on your own, and you'll see the results of a team effort, in long, medium and short term in terms of both profit and in terms of the advantages and new opportunity branches that you open up.

Ok, time for a real world example for you, and keep in mind this may well happen to you, whether it's a similar situation or under totally different circumstances. How did this very product come to exist? It all started a while back in the year 2000 when I joined a membership website by two big name marketers. Nothing major really went on, at the time I was spending most of my business day just talking to new people and testing marketing strategies for my own membership site.

Anyway, through just attending some of their consultations and participating in their community, as well as meeting these two big marketers, and several others, I also found myself in contact with big list owners and article writers. Bear in mind I wasn't actively seeking out any of this. Now at the time I didn't really see these people as an opportunity. I was just going with the flow really, meeting, greeting and talking to people in the same field of business as myself.

Not only did I end up starting sites with two of these people, and almost starting one with another (we decided it wasn't a viable idea in the end), but three years later, here's me happily managing my e-zine and websites, along comes a call from one of them that introduces me to yet more contacts. "I got this guy here, you may have heard of him, but he wants to set up this cool sounding site, but I don't have the time for it. Are you up for that?"

Sure I was, that sounds like a good new opportunity. Off I went, had a talk to with this new contact, who'd already been talking to the others I'd met through the same site. The result? This site, 500 sales within a few weeks, each paying us $500+ for our experience and to talk to our contacts first hand, and some real great new friends and business contacts to boot.

Don't get me wrong, this is just an example. Forget how much is earned and through who and when, I'm not trying to boast here, but what I am doing is really hammering this home. If you take nothing away from this site other than this report, I'd be happy in knowing how many options you've opened up for yourself and will again in the future. As long as you've picked up this number one point that opportunities are out there. It's a give and take process, and always mutually beneficial.

I should also point out at this point that what I just gave you was one example, one single example that bred 10+ new hard-hitting contacts. This has happened non stop since initial contact with people in my field of expertise. Just by talking, just by word of mouth, and just by me not trying to do everything on my own.

So let me ask you. Right now, are you working on your own? Are you open or closed to new contacts?

Next time something comes up that sounds good to you, don't pass it by and wonder what would have happened if you said yes. Do it, take it up on the spot and see where it takes you. Next time something comes up that sounds good to you, remember this story, and your wall painted with different coloured dots. Think about where different situations could take you and your business, and most of all, in a business environment, never expect something for nothing.

Kind of a mutual unsung rule, you scratch my back, I'll scratch yours. Remember also not to view everyone you meet as an opportunity for making wads more cash. I'm not about to test this, but I highly doubt it would do wonders for anybody's social life.

Where The Day Takes You

So when you wake up tomorrow, and every day from now on, and a new situation presents itself, think to yourself: Where could this take me? What new situations will arise right away, in a year, or even ten years later? Kind of like viewing your whole life up to this point as one big long line, one thing led to another, to another, to another, to another and so on. One thing I do need you to understand though to complete this concept is that you are in control.

Just like you drew those dots connecting your friends, and their friends' friends on the wall earlier, if you were to pick any one of them, do you think you could get yourself acquainted with just a few words through other friends? Too right you could, but it's up to you to take those steps, to choose where your line goes next, and to select who you're going to meet, and ultimately whether or not you're working towards being a success.

You want it to happen, you go and do it. Like I demonstrated earlier, understanding you have so much control, everything is in your hands and it's your choice is the first step to understanding how your going to move forward. This is totally relevant to your business, no matter how strange you may think this article is for an online marketing course. I need you to understand that you are in total control of what you're doing and what you're going to choose to do in the future.

Always create opportunities for yourself, leave your options open and you'll never be left stuck in a rut, or left with an unsolvable problem. Remember, the above example is an extreme one. Your aim isn't to use everyone you meet. Your aim is to do business as effectively as possible.

Don't be afraid to get involved.

Start Tomorrow and you will see results.

Action Points

• This section wasn't at all planned. I wanted to give you the essence of what's going on in my mind every day as I carry out my online marketing because, even though this is not a direct how to step by step guide, it's imperative that you understand this before going further.

• Something that I want you to try and do is keep an open mind throughout the whole course. Be open to new ideas and the new information that's coming your way. This is the only way that you'll get the best out of it and create an abundance of awesome ideas for your business.

• Myself not being a fan of positive thinking, this section is not related to that, but rather based around the concept, that it's not what you know, it's who you know.

• Have you ever woken up one morning and regretted missing an opportunity, or wondered why you didn't do something the previous night that you had the chance to do? How about in the longer term? Is there anything in the past that you wished you'd have done differently and that just maybe you might have been somewhere else doing something else because of that? If so, don't worry. Everyone has these missed opportunities and this section is all about making sure that never happens again.

• All day, every day new opportunities present themselves to us, and many don't even notice it happening. We need to wake you up and open your eyes to this happening around you right now, because ultimately it will lead to your success.

• The starting point is to understand that you shouldn't do everything on your own. I have never met anyone successful in the online marketing world that does not or has not at one time or another used this tactic to his or her advantage. If you want to be a success, from this point onwards, I want you to use it too.

• Sometimes you may feel that your goals, hopes and dreams are too far away for your liking, and it's frustrating because it's going to take too long to reach them. If we assume that the first step to being a success is about making contacts, scientifically, everything you want and could ever want is never more than seven steps away from you.

• An experiment I discovered recently showed a hermit living in isolated mountains in a far off country, and the challenge was to find someone from London, England, who knew him using seven steps. A friend of a friend, of a friend, of a friend, and it was a success.

• Understand right now that opportunities are out there. You need to open your mind, take a step back and pay attention. If you can do this, you'll start to see when and where opportunities are presenting themselves to you. All of which you want to be taking. The big business contact that could bring two or more of you mutual but massive success could be just a conversation away.

• I'm not saying you're going to wake up tomorrow with an e-mail in your inbox solving all your problems, but the potential to solve them is there. Opportunities in all shapes and forms are ripe and ready for picking, and if you don't do so, you'll miss out and someone else will take your spot.

• The power of the opportunity and contact making is immense. Lets imagine you're a budding new marketer who's made ten contacts by just being able to see these new opportunities arrive and meeting new business people. Ten times the income for all of you, ten times the promotion power, ten times the success. Can you meet ten people in the rest of your lifetime? If you answered yes, you can be a success.

• See how success isn't actually as far away as you may think. Imagine you're in a white room. Place a small dot on a wall; this dot is you. Now place a green dot next to you for friends you have, and next a blue dot for every friend they have and so on. Before long your room will be totally covered. Looking at this room full of dots, you can see how easy it is to start at the bottom of the line, and using this small scientific technique explained above, you have more potential than you ever dreamed of.

• On that same note, let me ask you, if you wanted to, could you get an introduction to your friends friend that you've never met before? I bet you could with a few words. The same is true with marketing. Everyone that you want to contact in the future for a mutually successful business relationship is right there and is reachable through someone you know. See how your success is closer than it appears?

• On top of this, for even more re-enforcement of how you can put this effect to good use, is to control it. What did you do when you just asked your friend earlier for an introduction to another friend? You controlled who you were meeting. How are you going to be a success in online marketing? Through the same scientific process of controlling where you want to go instead of waiting for opportunity to come to you.

• Opportunity can come in all shapes, forms and sizes, it doesn't have to be just meeting people. Use and apply this technique, take up everything you can as often as you can, and even though you can't predict where it's going to lead, at the end of it, you'll always have more than you started out with. This opportunity spotting and taking is the key to your success, plain and simple. (We'll also be talking more about this later, don't worry about specifics for now, just understand the concept, take it in, and know it exists)

• When you wake up tomorrow and any situation presents itself, any situation at all, think, where could this take me if I say yes, where could it take me if I do this instead of watching TV, who could I meet if I go here instead of taking an extra lie in after a late night. Remember your friends' dots that you drew on the wall?

• Where will this take you? Who knows, I don't know, you don't know, but one thing I can most definitely tell you without a doubt, is that it's going to take your forwards, towards your goals. Remember, you have the control here, no one else. It's in your hands and totally down to you. Always create options and opportunities for yourself in this way, and you'll never be stuck in a rut, not to mention how you'll immediately see your rapid forward movement in the direction that you want to be going in.

• Don't be afraid of change or new things. I need your full attention, dedication, and an open mind, that's all I ask of you. This alone will push you in the direction that you want to go in.

Success Overview
• To share the base need to know knowledge before moving on to specific & detailed online marketing techniques.

• To induce the correct mindset for success through answering three quick questions about yourself, instead of long drawn out positive thinking and goal setting processes.

• To make sure you know exactly what you're letting yourself in for, why you're doing this, where you are now, and where you want to be in the future.

• To decrease anxiety through opening up your mind to doing the opposite of what you've probably been doing for most of your life as far as deadline setting is concerned.

• To show you what to do with ideas for products or services that come to you that are not viable to complete at the present time.

• To lay down on the table the two most important things you should have in your mind and be carrying with you through everything you do related to your business.

• To explain how we as online marketers are all multi-skilled masters of creation, even if you don't feel that way.

• To demonstrate that it's far easier to move your business forwards, and in the direction you want it to go, than many have lead you to believe through other guides and scare tactics.

About Online Marketing

I'd like to take the time out to talk about what you're getting yourself into. Not just what you're getting yourself into, but what we've all dived in to headfirst; the fascinating world of online marketing.

Let me tell you, since 1999, I've seen a lot. I've seen people that seem to know almost everything, I've seen friends have amazing successes starting from the very bottom and working their way up. I've seen people succeed in achieving their dreams and goals, and I've seen people fail and just give up, not to mention, countless methods and guides for success, new systems of all sorts.

Looking back, it's been one heck of a ride with ups, downs, major ups and major downs. When I first got going with marketing I noticed something a little scary, and that was the high rate of failure. As I progressed building my business, testing my own methods, and moving up the ladder as it were, I started to realize things.

People were going about their online business totally blind to the fundamental flaws that they were creating for themselves. I started to look back at the people I'd met that had dropped out early on before achieving their goals and a few things started to jump out at me. I then decided that the day that I write an info product, the first things that I'm going to talk about are the fundamentals of business.

This is a really important section. In fact, I remember back in the day saying to myself 'When I make it and reach my goals, if I ever write an info product, I'm going to include a report entitled 'Things I Wish I Knew Before I started'. Everything you're about to read is very background like information. Things you should always have in your head while working your business. Kind of rules that you shouldn't deviate from, but aren't necessarily practical jobs that you can get on with right now.

Everything here I've seen and learnt at various stages of my business' development and would like to pass directly to you before we even get started to provide you with a base for your knowledge. Real facts that you should keep in mind while doing business online, or even offline, if you decide to go that way in the future.

The Basics of Online Success

The thing with online marketing is that anyone anywhere can start his or her own business. You don't need a huge amount of cash to put down for a property, and you don't need to buy stock, or put down a large sum of money for storage, and so on. This is great, but somewhere along the way, the basics of business have been forgotten.

Of course I won't bore you and relay everything that I learned in college and university, because to be honest, barely any of it applies to the real world of business. What I really want to get into in this section is you. Why you're doing what you're doing, what to expect, and most importantly how to go about this correctly on the ground floor, because of course building a strong base is extremely important for the short term, just in terms of survival, never mind total and utter success.

One thing that I find with online business is, people see the opportunity there to make a whole load of cash, quit their jobs and live the good life. In a way, this is true, but they forget about themselves. They see the money and their eyes light up. This is why I want to talk about you, what you want and how you plan to get it before going any further.

Why Are You Here?

First up, why are you here? Really ask yourself that question. Why have you decided to start your own business? Why online? Maybe it was the promise of some extra cash, a little extra free time. Do you want to go all the way and quit your job in the future? Or maybe you have some other motivation?

This is the basis of setting goals. Why are you here? When you've answered that question, remember it. Keep it filed, updated and well a truly embedded in your mind. Any tough times you come across, or any problems that may arise with your business in the future, remember why you're here and why you're doing this and why it is worthwhile. The answer to this question is what's going to spur you on and keep you going and moving on up the ladder.

Some people like to create whole elaborate plans around their goals, but for now we'll leave it at that. Quick and simple. It's not hard, it's not time consuming but it is an extremely important part of your success. All you ever need to do is ask yourself those three questions. Why am I here? What do I want? How do I plan to get it? Basic? You may think so, but look at it this way, without this motivation, you may find yourself waking up in five years' time, sitting in the same chair, in the same place, in the same situation and wondering why you haven't moved forward. It's likely because you didn't set yourself a goal, which is done simply by answering those three questions. Don't let this happen to you.

This Is Real Business

Next up, I want to touch on something that I still see every day, and to be honest, it does make me wonder. I want you to remember what you're doing here. You're starting or building a business. The problem I see every day is, as we already mentioned earlier, the opportunity is there for everyone, but it doesn't seem to sink in that they're actually starting their own business.

I can understand how you'd be a little miffed about someone starting a business that didn't know they were doing so, but let me explain. I'm sure you've seen those websites with links all over the place, totally disorganized, a page full of pretty colors telling you click on one and you'll earn thousands of dollars an hour, or a lovely free hosted site with ten pop ups on each page and a pretty floral border with bright pink animated background of happy little bunnies prancing around the place.

It's not just the layout of sites either, it's the customer service, the quality of the sales letters, the quality of the product, the price, the presentation, everything, every single aspect.

It really makes me think when I land on these pages. Do these guys know that they're supposed to be running a business? Don't hate me yet; I know that sounds very opinionated, but its roots are based in fact. Would you buy from these sites even if the product sounded totally amazingly great? I sure wouldn't. There are too many things on my mind. Too many questions I have to ask myself.

A good marketer knows that as well as having a good product, the worries of any visitor to your website need to be squashed as quickly as possible. All the questions you ask yourself before buying something about the person that's selling to you and the product itself need to be answered and answered well, or you're just going to click off and move along. The major point I'm trying to make here is understand fully what you're getting yourself into. With the anonymity of internet and the people selling products on it, you have to remember above all to be business like and professional at all times. If you create something and don't feel totally comfortable with it, chances are it's not up to scratch and it's not going to do you any favours, money wise, free time wise, long term, or short term.

Here's a good example. During the planning stages, this very report that you're reading has gone through no less than six drafts and different versions because it wasn't good enough. It wasn't professional enough, it didn't hit home the points strongly enough. This site has gone through many small changes, including three designs, one total overhaul, four versions of the scripts running in the background, two different affiliate scripts and some custom work.

I'm not saying you have to go overboard, but my personal belief, based in fact is that if you have put in the extra effort with something, customers will notice, and they will remember you, most importantly though, they will buy from you in the first place. Always, always keep your work professional and top quality if you want to get off the starting blocks, or it just won't happen for you.

Your Personality Gets You Noticed
Here comes the fun part. Taking the above idea of being professional at all times, you may feel that this next point is a contradiction in terms, and that is, inject your own personality. This is really important for the success of any online business, and it sure helps get to know people and meet new contacts and form business relationships.

Professionalism is all good, but on its own, it's just not enough. I see this more and more, every day with the e-zines I get through my mail, the reports I'm sent by people, and the sales letters for new products or services that I read on a daily basis.

As far as I'm concerned right now, you're reading this, and having read the introduction so far, you have some insight into us and who we are, what we sound like and it gives the course some personality. You know the source of them. If we didn't do this, you would just be reading another boring bundle of text that didn't have any background or meaning.

Here's a slightly more direct example for you. Right now, and throughout the rest of the course, I'm writing to you, and talking to you as if I was talking to a friend, but in a professional sense. We didn't want to create a tedious experience for you, otherwise it'd turn into another random and boring faceless block of text telling you what to do, and that's the last thing we want. We'd lose out, and you'd lose out, get bored, stop reading, and take away a negative experience with our names attached to it. Not good, not good for either of us.

I'm sure you're getting the idea now, keep that in mind when you're writing your own sales letters, your own reports, publishing your e-zine, creating your info product or membership site, in fact keep it in mind whatever you're doing, alongside the professionalism. Remember, being a professional and respected businessman or businesswoman doesn't mean you have to go about your work in a boring way. Inject your own personality. It will not only help people remember you and build your personal brand, as well as your business, but it will keep your customers reading and coming back to you for more.

Your Personal Resource Reserve

The next important section I want to talk about is your resources. How much time do you have to devote? Do you need more? How much cash do you have to put down? Do you need more? In this short introduction section, just for examples purposes, I'm going to give you some insight as to my own personal working time table and how much cash I spend on what, so that you can see how similar products sometimes require diverse panning and bring up very different situations.

Something that's very important to me here is that in light of the last section on professionalism, you don't misunderstand what I'm showing you as 'do everything a hundred times over and spend a week on every little section until it's perfect'. Every single product and service that you create, or decide to sell for someone else is going to bring it's own revelations with regards to cost and the time out of your schedule that it takes and this is something very important that should be taken into account in the planning process, because lets face it, you don't want to find yourself three quarters of the way through a product, just to find out that you've run out of time or cash.

Here's an example of my personal schedule for you. Bear in mind that my business is my job, and I don't do any outside work aside from freelance affiliate promotion for others. For this reason, I don't expect you to follow this, or ours to be the same. This is here for one reason only, and that's to give you a heads up. Ok so, week one, I'll do general admin work of the business and sites, keep on top of accounts, make a few new contacts and generally talk to a lot to people and current customers. Read feedback, make small adjustments and so on, less than an hour a day if I can help it.

Week two; along comes one of the contacts I made last week who suggests an idea for a new site. This is where things go crazy and I'll spend pretty much the whole of the week and every spare hour planning and crafting this product and it's sales material, the follow-up, site graphics and preparing any scripts etc.

Week three comes the launch, and aside from spending a few hours a day on admin duty and making sure everything is functioning correctly, and arranging, preparing and getting the launch promotion drive going, this is all that's going on.

Week four, with everything running smoothly again it's back to the admin, meeting people and planning new products, and analysing and, most importantly, improving the way things are at the moment. This process of easy laid back work, onto major hard time consuming stuff, then back to the slower pace seems to be a pretty regular pattern you can rely on when creating your own sites.

Here's another example for you. The secondary affiliate promotion that I do with other people, removing the need to create my own products takes a big chunk out of that time. I may spend an hour or two a day in total creating promotions for others, writing new ad material and general business admin, but that's it.

When you consider not all websites that you create have a time limit, which is especially apparent when creating sites with a partner we've done with this one, and you can spread that work load out over the course of a week, two weeks, a month or maybe more, the answers to 'How much time does it take?' is easy; as much time as you can spare.
What I want to show is that something that could seem too huge to comprehend having the time for to start with can be spread out over time. Creating your own products does take longer. However, I don't want you to think that you're restricted to affiliate promotion just because you have other real life engagements such as work. This is by far not the case, and something that you have to pick up on right now if you're going to be a success when we move onto the practical sections.

The same is true for the financial side of things. How much cash does it take to start an online business? Well, to be honest, not a lot. You could easily get going for maybe $50. Get a website, create a product and get hosted.

I want you to know though, that you're not gated from creating something big, something profitable and a business to be proud of because of small time constraints or budgetary concerns. A little of each is good to start out with.

How Much Money Will You Make?
Next up something that we all enjoy talking about - Money. Not money you're spending however, but how much you are going to earn with your business? This is something that's no doubt of at least some importance to everyone reading right now. Let's talk cash. I'm sure you've seen all the big marketers out there earning huge wads of cash, hundreds of thousands of dollars a year and so on. I'm also sure you've heard or seen many people struggling to make just five hundred dollars per month too.

All too often I see too many marketers trying to fit into the top group when they're really in the bottom group, kind of like climbing a ladder, but totally missing out the middle rungs. Don't worry yourself too much. There is an 'in the middle'. As much as some sales letters would like you to not believe this is so.

You've Got All the Time in the World
I know many people that earn between thirty and eighty thousand dollars a year. They're not super rich, but again they have a great base to work from. My point here is don't set yourself a target of earning a million dollars a year within six months. This isn't to say it can't happen, this isn't to say it can't happen real quickly, but you have to stop setting yourself time limits, because all it does is add to your frustration and anxiety of only having so many days or weeks left to reach your goals. Just work towards it, and you will get there. Throw all your time limits out the window right this moment.

Don't try to be the richest person out there. Remember the first point we talked about? Why are you doing this? This is your primary goal, and don't be downhearted if you're not as rich as you hoped within the first few months. To sum up, you will earn as much as you want to earn if you take the professionalism point into account at every turn. Whether it's a thousand a month, a thousand a week, or a thousand a day, I want to reassure you now that it is achievable and you're not wasting your time reading this, but if you're going to make it, you need to stop setting yourself deadlines right now.

Why We're All Special
The fourth fundamental I want to talk to you about is generally only related to online business, and not so much for off-line business. That is about our skills. You may not think it if you've been on the scene a while, but we're special. Yep, you are. All of us are special in that we are so skilled and probably don't even notice it. Take a look at what creating the average product takes us through.

We Plan the product, we create a product, we design and build a website and we get it hosted, we set up affiliate programs, payment processors. We write our own sales material, we advertise our own products, we maintain our own lists, follow-up, backend sales, business admin, and customer service. You name it. We do it.

Granted you can have web designers build your graphics for you, copywriters write your sales material and so on, but if you're just starting out and don't have that kind of cash to spend, it all falls to you.

This isn't a problem, but the one thing I want to get across to you before moving on to the next sections is to keep things structured. Information overload is bad, and if you try to be the best at everything, you'll end up tired, run down, confused and probably still no better off. Go easy on yourself.

Here's a nice example for you. My specialty definitely isn't designing graphics for websites, (far from it, believe me) which is exactly why I hired someone to do this one for us. It didn't cost a huge amount, the whole site in fact, aside from the built in affiliate system, cost under three hundred dollars.

The above example included the whole of the members area, the log in system, the graphics, and outside the members' area, so that's not a bad deal. This is true for every skill we have and obtain. If you have the skill go for it, if you have the cash and you're not so good (like my design skills) hire someone.

My second point here is it's very rare that you'll want to have something done and there isn't someone out there to do it for you if you can't do it yourself. Don't give up on ideas because they seem too out of your league.

Ok one final point to make before we finish with today. It is all worth it. Whether it's more money you're after, or more time to spend with your family, there is a business size, type or way of doing things that suits you. The above section may have seemed a little messy and a little jumpy as far as subjects are concerned, however, if someone took my business away today, and told me to start again, they would be the number one things I'd be happy to know this time around, that weren't so apparent last time.

If the reasoning behind this report isn't immediately clear, let me explain. If you really did look at yourself, everything you want to achieve, everything you're doing, have done and will do, I now know for sure you are 100% totally and completely comfortable with your position. You know where you're going. You know in a very general format how you're going to get there, and you also know what you're capable of.

If some things are still unclear, feel free to go over the report again, but this time really ask yourself the questions and have answers before moving onto the next one.

A space filler this is not. Read it over again if you have to, or maybe at a later date. Everything here is I believe a great base of knowledge for your business. Want proof? Try it, and watch what happens.

Action Points

• It's important to understand all of these ideas before diving headfirst into creating your own business. If we're going to be successful at anything we need some background information first, and to understand how it works.

• Online Marketing is no exception. I've seen many things, lots of ups and downs. Amazing successes, massive bankrupting failures, I've seen, read and indeed own masses of guides, how to's, and online marketing information.

• One of the main problems is, people were going about their business totally blind to the fundamental flaws of what they were creating for themselves. This was easy to see by examining the people that had failed and comparing them with the people that succeeded on my journey here. This is when I decided when I reach my goals, I'm going to write a course based around the title: Things I wish I knew before I got started. This is that course.

• Nowadays anyone can start their own business online. All they need is an idea, and a very small amount of cash. There's no longer any need for large amounts of investment. Looking around, it's obvious to me that for this reason people forget that they're running a business, and just look at it as a quick way to make some extra cash. Let me tell you now, you are a businessman, or businesswoman. Never forget that.

• No matter how much people don't like the whole positive thinking and goal setting frame of mind, you have to do it. Goal setting at least, because this is going to be your driving motion that's going to push you towards success. No goals means no motivation, no motivation means waking up in five years time and wondering why you're in the same place. Similarly, no set goals means chasing something that you want that's always getting bigger and better, and further away, which means you'll never reach it. You need a set goal.

• Setting yourself some goals doesn't involve positive thinking, it's not a lot of work either. It just requires you to answer a few questions. Think about these right now. Why are you here, and why are you doing what you're doing right now? What do you want to get out what you're doing right now? This is all goal setting requires. Nothing boring, nothing elaborate, but it's the difference between you moving forward, and staying where you are right now.

• Coming across tough times or a problem that you don't know how to solve? Not a problem, refer back to your goal for some motivation. Why are you here? What are you doing right now? And what do you want to get out of what you're doing right now? That's all it takes, nothing more.

• It has to sink in that you're starting or building your own business. This is not a game; this is not a toy, or something for you to show your friends. It's entirely your creation, and it's there for one reason and one reason only, and that is to achieve your goals and improve your life.

• It sometimes makes me wonder if people realise what they're getting in to. Professionalism is a must at all times. I'm sure you've seen the sites packed with affiliate links, pink fluffy floral borders with bright flashing lights that talk to you about making millions overnight. It makes me wonder, do these people even know that they're running a business? Would you buy from these sites even if the product sounded like the best thing ever to land on the Internet?

• It's not about site design either. It's about professionalism. You have to have this with you in everything you do. It has to be the best work you've ever done. When I say everything I'm talking your marketing, your joint ventures, your sales letters, your ad copy, your follow-up, your product, your affiliate system, any contact that you make with your list or any other resources you may have, in fact anything and everything that you're going to do that's related to your business.

• A good marketer knows that as well as having a good product, to make any sales at all; they have to eliminate any worry from the customers mind when they land on your sales letters. These need to be squashed as quickly as possible. Without this level of professionalism it just won't happen for you. Always think business, always think business owner, and always think one hundred and ten percent professionalism if you're seriously looking to get anywhere.

• For example, take this product. It's gone through six drafts and several planning stages over a period of time, simply because it wasn't good enough when it started out. It wasn't professional enough, and it didn't hit home the points strongly enough.

• Don't go overboard with this, otherwise you will never get anything done, but keep it with you, keep it at the front of your mind at all times and you'll do just fine.

• Inject your personality. This may sound like a contradiction in terms from the above advice that I gave you about being professional, however, being professional on it's own just doesn't cut it. If you want to stand out, if you want to be noticed and remembered, I don't want you to be afraid to put a little of yourself in there. After all, if you're remembered, you're trusted. If you're trusted, you'll make a bundle more sales.

• Being professional doesn't mean being boring. For example this report, I'm talking to you as if I were talking to a friend. You're getting a whole bundle of information and a little bit of me at the same time, something it's unlikely you'll be forgetting in a hurry. Keep this alongside your professionalism.

• Think about your resources. How much time do you have? Do you need more? The answer is you can put in as much time as you have to spare, even if it's just seven hours a week to start with. You can spread the work over a longer period of time. Don't throw a good idea out the window just because you can't finish it in a few days. You're not gated from creating a cracking product just because you don't have masses of time to spare or have budgetary concerns.

• Try not to get frustrated because you're not rich. There is more to this than being rich and broke, and in monetary terms there are plenty of comfortable in the middle stages, where you may not have reached your goals yet, but you sure are moving towards them and in a much better position compared to when you started.

• Don't get too hung up on setting yourself deadlines. Deadlines equal anxiety, frustration, and will slow you down. Set a goal and work towards it, and you will get there.

• We are all special. Jack-of-all-trades, we don't have a massive staffing base to do stuff for us. We write our own sales material, we advertise our own products, we maintain our own lists, follow-up, backend sales, business admin, and customer service. You name it. We do it.

• You will pick up many skills along the way, but again, don't throw away an idea just because you don't know how to do something. It's highly likely there's going to be someone out there that you can hire for parts of the project that you can't do. For example, I 'm terrible at designing website graphics but that doesn't mean I stopped putting sites up. I learned at the start, and nowadays have someone to do this for me.

• Congratulations, because if you can now answer the three questions: What am I doing here? Why am I doing it? What do I hope to achieve? Then you're in the prime mindset to continue. We're both on the same page for maximum efficiency, and more importantly, probably without even noticing it, just by doing this, in the past thirty minutes of the course, you've started to move forwards already. Let's keep it going.

Action Points
• To discuss the top reasons for success and failure, to try and identify any of these features in the way you work and to stamp them out before we get into the serious promotion of your product later in this area.

• To show you that no matter how good any previous guides sounded, if you followed them, and they didn't work, they weren't telling you the whole story.

• To demonstrate that you probably know more about online marketing than you think.

• To talk about the way we all spend our day and our routines as self employed, and how a simple problem with the transition from skivvy to complete control could be holding you back.

• To show you that there are always parts of online marketing that someone doesn't enjoy, and to give you a heads up on the number one reason that this could be stopping you dead in your tracks.

• To discuss previous advice and guides that you may have read and what some marketers will tell you to get you to listen to them. If they're telling you a particular phrase which has become all the rage lately, no matter how nice and kind they are to you, they can't help you.

• To show you how to move on and how not moving on could leave you maintaining the same product for years to come with very little profit. In my experience a very common mistake, I also landed in this sticky trap.

Top 10 Reasons for Success

Greetings, welcome to the section where we'll be looking at some of the reasons why some are successful and some are not. There are a lot of reasons why this may occur. I want to talk through with you some of the most common, and some of the problems I had to overcome myself on my way here and that many others that I've spoken to also had to overcome. Rather than being a totally negative report in which I tell you why you're not being as successful as you'd like, let's look at this in a different light. I'm going to show you as many reasons as I can think of why marketers are struggling so that you can actively spot and solve them immediately.

Many are struggling, it's a fact, through a plethora of situations through no fault of their own. After all, this isn't something you can go to school or to college for and be taught. When we start out we're all feeling our way in the dark, and mistakes will be made, this is a guarantee.

Whilst reading through I'd like you to really focus on what's being said and be on the look out for examples that sound like you, or something you might do. It's nothing to be embarrassed about, nothing to get aggravated or annoyed about, it's solely something for you to think 'wow, that sounds like me, I best quit that.' That's the exact effect we're looking for here, nothing more.

So without further delay, let's start looking at some of the reasons some marketers are more successful than others and some of the solutions if you're having a particular problem.

Are You Listening to the Right People?

The first one I'd like to talk to you about is your choice of guide purchasing. Granted this doesn't apply now because you've taken the plunge, but did you ever feel like someone wasn't quite telling the whole story with previous guides you've purchased or even been given?

It's all too easy to find information about online marketing, but whether that information is good, tried, tested and complete is another matter altogether. Often, when people start out, they tell me that they've been reading this free e-book they were given, and what I'm telling them contradicts what's been written, or they read about something before but were never sure how to actually go about doing things. Generally, the more you spend the better quality you get.

It's unfortunate that many marketers on the outside of reports such as these don't understand that they're not being told the whole story, or even being told incorrect information.

Don't get me wrong I'm not knocking smaller products but understand if you want a guide that shows you all the tips and trade secrets it sure isn't going to cost you $25. If you have any friends in the business, or anyone you know to be making this mistake, point it out to them. Unfortunately, trying to point someone to a high priced product is not always easy to do, because it just sounds like sales talk, but I digress, let's move on.

I Bet You Know More Than You Think
Big reason number two, is you already knew how to do everything but didn't get the work done for some reason. There are plenty of reasons for this, but let me say I experienced this one too, until one day I bought someone else's product which kind of put me straight, and got me thinking. Hey this guy is big and makes a load of cash, but already knows everything he is teaching. This spurred me on quite nicely and turned out to be the boost I needed to get to this stage, selling multiple $1000+ products daily for several months of the year. It was a great motivator and sometimes that's just what people need to spring into action again, not necessarily the knowledge itself. This is something I kept in mind with this report, and the reason we have the goal pages and summaries at the end of the written versions. I'd hope they did their job, made you feel as though you were progressing and learning new methods and techniques that would be useful to you. I'd suggest doing something similar with your products too.

Wasting Time without Even Knowing It
Moving on, you know, it's amazing how much time we waste doing nothing useful even when it seems we are. Someone pointed this out to me four or five years ago and said hey, I have something for you to test. Next time you're doing a big job such as writing a report, or building a site, record how much work you do, how much you get done over how much time, then report back to me in the morning. I guarantee you I can triple the amount you got done without sacrificing quality the next day. Intrigued I did as she said. Came back the next day and she demonstrated to me how much time I was wasting doing irrelevant things. Either catching news reports on TV, going to grab some food, speak to some friends for a few minutes, flick through the tracks on my MP3 player between each song trying to find the good ones and so on.

Here's another more recent example of this. I've been working on this report now and some software at the same time for many months. I just sat down for seven hours straight (something I can rarely do with the number of projects I'm working on currently) and wrote, and wrote, and came out with 60+ pages, which means if I'd really sat down and concentrated on the one project I'd have had 1200+ pages done in a mere 20 days. So here's the thing. When you work try to either, keep a timetable, a set of goals, or at the very least a record of how much you're achieving and cut out all distractions.

Don't get me wrong, I'm not calling you lazy. I know you want to move forward or else you wouldn't be reading this right now. Take some time out to work on your business. Sit down, remove all distractions and just work, straight, for 12 hours. Taking a look around on my desk now I have my headphones on, with set play list going, I have my keyboard, a watch, and a glass of iced water. That's it, nothing more. The best thing about this is there are no distractions, and I get work done. I'd suggest at the very least you might want to draw up a timetable for your work days, and set yourself goals to avoid this. It's amazing how time flies and the work amount and quality is affected through distractions. Try it, you might just find the pace of things pick up.

Does This Sound Like You?
Next up comes 'the avoid' the dirty bits way of thinking. Have you ever been sitting there, maybe working away or reading your guides on how to achieve something, and said to yourself 'Hmm you know, I don't fancy doing that', or 'This is not what I envisioned doing when I started out in online marketing'? Well you wouldn't be the only one and this could well be the missing piece of the puzzle for you. In general when you start to delve deep into this business it's very different from what you see on the outside. Not only that, but things can change.

Unfortunately we as online marketers have to take the good with the bad and carry on regardless. This sometimes results in coming up against something that will require you to overcome a barrier or pull of something new. Usually when I talk to people about their online marketing the number one thing that comes up here is joint ventures. Especially the first time around because you're no longer dealing with masses of lists, but on a personal level and, it can indeed be a little hard to get going if you've never done it before. As I mentioned earlier they don't teach you this stuff in college or universities.

So here's the thing. You need to look at everything you're doing relating to your business and ask yourself whether it's helping or hindering you. When you find an answer, be it in this report, or elsewhere, if you don't like the idea of having to do it yourself, either hire someone to do it if you can, or if not, it's time to burn some bridges. Whatever you do don't block it out and put it to the back of your mind figuring that that one small thing that you've left out won't make that much difference. In my experience everything you do is chained to something else. Leaving one out can leave you with a huge gap in your online marketing.

Don't Listen to the Big Guys...

Moving on to the next and probably the most worrying part of this report, and that's that you may have found yourself a 'don't listen to the big guys' person, or a report written by such a person. This confuses me to this day. The usual argument is they're only in it for themselves, so don't listen to them, listen to me instead because I'm a nice person. Now I don't know how many people go for this to be honest, but guru bashing as I like to call, it seems to have become a popular business proposition for some people.

Don't buy it. That's like telling you not to listen to the people that are making the money, but to listen to the person that doesn't listen to the people making the money. Strange. My retort to the guru bashing is, no, they're not just in it for themselves. If I were to put this report out and leave in a shoddy condition, and make a few hundred sales just because I can write a sales letter, I'd love to see how many people come back and buy from me later or promote my products. No one would want to be associated with me, I wouldn't get joint ventures, I wouldn't sell any products and so on. Not only me, it's kind of an unwritten rule out there.

You make it good, or you don't make it at all.

Broken Vase Syndrome

Next, something that personally stopped me from moving on for a year or so. I had this old site going that was doing pretty well, considering I hadn't learned much at that period. It wasn't a small site by any means. I was forever updating, changing, prettying up, cleaning, tidying, maintaining and so on. Meanwhile, someone I'd met about the same time I started out in online marketing pulled three sites out of the bag. I was wondering how he did it. We knew each other anyway so he'd given me access to his sites and I was amazed. They weren't lacking in content, they were good solid, full blown websites.

I remember talking to him one day and he said to me 'Hey, you've been working on that site for a long time haven't you, it must be pretty huge by now'. Yeah it was, I thought to myself at the time, but I totally missed the point. There comes a time after you release a product when you should have everything set up and running nicely so that you're free to move on to a new product. Never constrain yourself to one and work on it constantly over huge periods of time. If you find yourself doing this you're doing something wrong.

Understand that there's nothing wrong with keeping up customer support for your products, but set it up, finish up and get promoting. Smooth everything over as quickly as possible and to the best of your abilities. This is especially true for info based products but even with software you need to automate and move on, not totally leaving it behind, but leaving it to run itself for the most part.

Keep an open mind, work on new products and new projects, and don't get stuck doing one thing for years whilst your competition has released ten products and is raking it in from them, whilst you're still with your original site re-arranging its layout or scheme.

The moment I discovered this it kind of set me free, and here I am now working on a monstrous amount of projects with more contacts, a bigger list and more knowledge in my head than I ever imagined would fit. Unfortunately some of the people I knew back in those days weren't all that lucky and, are still in pre-launch for a product they created four years ago, earning no more than they did in the first week or so. Each to their own. I highly suggest you keep an open mind though and know when it's time to move on to bigger, better and newer things.

I'm Worried I Can't / Won't Succeed

Next up comes something that's not unrelated to what we spoke about earlier, when looking at avoiding the dirty bits, and that's worrying about not succeeding. Now you may not be the type of person to worry about what other people are thinking or how they'll react to your products and the things you do, which is great, because you'll burn bridges a lot faster than us out there that hate it when someone doesn't like our work. This is why you'll always get the best from anything I do personally, but for those of you who are reading and who get a little uptight when approaching something new this is for you.

The fact is, if you're in online marketing or any business that I've encountered so far, you'll need to burn bridges and try something new every now and again, and carry out tasks that you don't feel comfortable with or are going to really despise doing. Let me tell you, as the kind of guy that likes to please everyone all the time, I understand that it's not easy when you come up against things like this. I've been sworn at, shouted at, refused, denied, flat out told things I've done were crap, useless, don't work and so on. I don't doubt I'll get the same again in the future from people who can't be bothered to get out there and try these methods, and you know what? If you haven't experienced all this already, let me tell you now that you will.

Way to make you feel better huh? Well now you know, and you're prepared for it, you have to accept it and move on. You'll need to find your own way of getting by and not being discouraged when something goes incredibly pear shaped. Whatever you do though, always push yourself to break new boundaries and, don't let anything discourage you because what you don't see when people tell you they make 20k a month is that they're getting this too. Each and every one of them. Whether it's from their list, the odd strange customer, or just someone having a bad day. You will encounter it, so prepare to get over it now and you'll be fine. Those of you more laid back who don't get dented by that stuff, great. Keep moving forward.

Knowledge Really Is Power

Next up, we have the all important knowledge. Knowledge is power, after all, and without it we'd all be doomed and useless at pretty much everything. Well you don't have to worry about not having the knowledge anymore because everything is covered in this guide for this particular method, but I do want you to make sure you're using it. The whole buying guide, after guide, after guide is getting a little over the top for some people that I've spoken to in the past. Ten, twenty, thirty or more e-books read. They claim they've read everything but still haven't reached their dream of making wads of cash every month.

Like we've already discussed this can be for many reasons. You can have all the knowledge in the world but it won't do anything unless you take what you've learned and put it to good use. Don't turn into one of those report hoppers, because it won't get you very far, and in the end you're going to end up frustrated, bored and broke.

The Freebie Magnet
Next we have the freebie magnet. Seeing as anyone reading this will have purchased it, I highly doubt this applies, but I want to be sure and catch anyone right here and weed these problems out before they start. This comes in many forms but I want to talk about this in general rather than anything specific as in the other sections. So free stuff. We all like something for nothing but there are those people out there who go over the top searching for free deals. Free hosting, free promotion, free web design, free sales copy writing and so on. It just doesn't work. You will not get anything set up if you're looking for everything that's free. Granted, shop around for a good deal if you can, but when it comes to the fundamentals of your business, your scripts, your hosting especially, don't go with the free option because quality will suffer, and your customers will be able to see that too, which is something we definitely want to avoid.

I highly doubt many of you are here buying such a product so I won't dwell. I thought it best to cover it just in case and for future reference. So swiftly moving along and we hit a wall that is suffered by many marketers out there.

Never On Your Own
This brings me to my next point and that's don't try to do everything on your own. A big mistake many marketers make is that they decide that they want all the profits for themselves and try to do everything alone. This is all well and good if you want to be making a couple of thousand a month maybe but if you want to surpass that you need to expand a little. That's not to say that you need to go around partnering on every single site that you create but it does mean that you need to think a little more about working in a team wherever possible.

Partnerships are one example and you'll be splitting the profits 50/50. However lets say for example you both have the same amount of resources to get your promotion out through different contacts and each others lists, affiliates, Jv's and customers, mix in a little bit of your expertise and you'll end up making the same amount of cash anyway if things are dead even. What you will get though are double the visitors, double the people in your follow-up, and double your affiliates adding fifty percent to your total income from the product to start with. On top of that you'll be pulling in double the resources to promote to in the future.

So you see it's important to start working as a team. Don't worry if you haven't got anyone to work in a team with yet. After your first few products you'll start to see some contacts land in your lap that you can join up with later. There is another example of this and that's when people don't want to grant affiliate commissions because they don't want to be losing any cash. I can totally understand it if you have a huge amount of resources already, but when you don't have that type of promotion power under your belt, affiliates are the way to go.

Affiliates, however, are here to stay, and they'll be the difference between your 1k a month and your 20k a month and upwards. Remember, affiliates are making sales that it's likely you wouldn't have made anyway, so there's nothing wrong with granting them more out of the profits than you're earning per sale. If you have a problem doing this you're going to struggle so, if this really isn't something you want to do, take some time out and check how much you'd be earning if you gave 60% to say ten affiliates making a particular number of sales on your product on top of your personal sales. You should start to see how much more profitable this is than trying to go it alone, which is both time consuming and expensive, cutting into your profits big time unless you use these resources for the leverage you need to make your one person promotion team into a ten, a hundred or even thousand plus person promotion team. It's at this stage this point really starts to become clear.

So there we have it. The top reasons that I believe get in the way of marketers goals and stop them from succeeding. Do you see any of these in yourself? If you do, remove them, or fix them. It doesn't matter how you do it, just make sure you do, because they will hold you back and in all of the examples above will stop you from ever succeeding unless you can overcome them.

It's a fact that we as online marketers as I've mentioned before have to be multi skilled. When you get into the scene it's very, very rare and unlikely that you'll have everything you need to succeed, and there will be many problems, walls and obstacles that you have to personally overcome before you can make a success of this. You see, us marketers are all a little box of versatility, (you included). This is the most powerful of any tool at our disposal and will make us all successes. Unfortunately as much good as it does for those of us who understand this, it's detrimental to those who don't, and they will go on buying and buying guide after guide, getting frustrated and failing until they either quit, or learn this.

Well, I hope you enjoyed this report. It is indeed the most negative of them all, and I prefer to concentrate on success rather than why people fail. Alas it had to be done and was too important to leave out and not tell you about. We'll end here now, but before we do, I just want to make a note. If none of the above apply to you right now that's great. Take the knowledge contained within this report, put it to good use, and I look forward to seeing many successful products come from you. Be careful though, just because you don't have these problems right now, you may develop any of them later. Don't forget what you've just been reading and you'll do just fine.

Action Points

- Greetings, welcome to the section where we'll be discussing why some people are successful and why some aren't, drawing from the primary factors that went into the failures and successes of all the people that I personally met on the way. That came and went, that failed and quit, that succeeded and quit their jobs and bought ridiculously large houses and expensive cars.

- There are many different reasons for success, and everyone is different, but what I'd like to concentrate on now are two simple questions that I ask almost everyone I meet when they reach the peak of their marketing, whether it be success or failure. Why do you think you didn't make it? And of course, why do you think you made it? You'd be surprised at the results, I sure was. Let's look at this information now.

- The first thing I'd like to talk about is your choice of guide purchases. This one doesn't apply so much now seeing as you have this in your hands but it's definitely something I'd like you to watch out for in the future.

- All too often when people are starting out they'll tell me they've been reading this free e-book or they've visited this free site. They've pulled a load of info from it, and what I'm telling them to do, and what other marketers are telling them to do contradicts what they've been told by wherever they were previously. The general rule is the more you spend, the better you get.

- I'm not denying that small courses and cheap courses can be useful, and I'm not saying what I'm teaching you here is the be all and end all of information and the only way to be a success, but understand if you want a guide that really shows you solid marketing information, someone isn't going to reveal all of their best tactics for free.

- So my advice to you would be to always look for premium products if you want the full story. I doubt anyone would even consider selling a guide costing more than five hundred dollars if it was all shoddy. It would be devastating to their business, and isn't something buyers will forget in a hurry. Similarly, if you have any friends or make any contacts relying on small e-books for their marketing information, let them know that premium products are the way to go. Not necessarily this guide, I'm not trying to get you to go selling for me, but any well known marketer with a premium product is their best bet if they want to learn new things and serious techniques. Remember not to hard sell them just point them in the right direction in a friendly manner. It's in your best interests if your marketing contacts and customers succeed.

- Moving on to the second thing that I have personally seen and even experienced myself, which came very close to adding me to the list of those who didn't make it, and that's that you already have all the information and know how, but don't realize it, and therefore don't feel comfortable putting it into action for one reason or another.

• My personal experience of this was a bit of a shock. I spent just over a grand buying a big marketers product that claimed to reveal all his secrets. On reading I found myself thinking, hey, this guy knows a lot, he makes a whole bundle of cash, but I already know literally everything that he's telling me. I found myself adding more to his tips in my mind while reading through, kind of unconsciously saying 'Hey, you missed a bit'.

• At this point I realized it was time to start moving forward and taking action. The initial learning period was over. Watch for this because you may find you know more than you think, and your success could well just be a matter of you taking the plunge and confidently putting all you've learned into action.

• In addition to this the progression from the worker to the boss isn't the easiest thing to do by far, a common misunderstanding, and something else that got me for a period back in 2002. The way this one hit me was that a friend came to me and said 'next time you're working on your business, or doing a big job, record how much time you spend doing it and how much you get done, then report back to me, and he guaranteed I could triple this through a simple fifteen minutes of easy work. I did as she said, and when I returned she demonstrated how much time was being wasted, catching the news, flipping through songs to listen to while I'm working, grabbing food, speaking to some friends, making calls and so on.

• So here's the thing. When you work try to either keep a timetable if that's your thing, a set of goals for the day in list format, or at the very least keep a record of the amount of work you're getting done and cut out the distractions totally. It sounds minor, I know, but try it and see how much more you get done when writing your reports. Being lazy doesn't come into it. It's all about that transgression to being in total control. Don't let anyone ever tell you that it's easy because it sure does take some getting used to.

• Taking a look around on my desk now, I have my headphones on with a set play list going, I have my keyboard, a watch and a glass of iced water. That's it. It's amazing how time flies and how work quality is affected by distractions. Remove them and prosper.

• Moving on from distractions the next thing I want to talk to you about is avoicing the dirty bits, a way of thinking that is in my experience affecting almost every marketer in their first six months of serious hard online marketing.

• Ever learned something new and thought to yourself, ah well I can skip this bit and do it later, or this isn't really how I pictured this to be? It happens to everyone, and when you have a pre-determined picture of how something should be in your head, it's hard to go about something that you don't enjoy totally. It's even easier to avoid things when you're in total control as with your own business.

• For example, when I started out in online marketing I thought it'd be all about posting paid ads, creating products and getting paid. Of course it didn't work out like that, and it turns out that pulling new Joint Ventures and making first contact with people isn't my forte, whilst the creative side and product creation totally is. What would happen if JV's were totally ignored, or I'd edited the techniques I'd learned in my mind down to only doing the things I enjoy the most? Well, personally I'd have been back selling other peoples stuff pretty quick.

• So the first thing I'd like you to do now is open your mind, and ask yourself, "is there anything that I've been avoiding doing because it doesn't fit into my pre-conceptions of what running a business and online marketing is about?".

• Dig deep and answer truthfully, because you may already have the key that you need to be a success. You just may not know it because it's been placed at the back of your mind as something you don't particularly want to do, or edited out of your personal knowledge base because it's something you're not prepared to do. If you find an answer to that question, bring it to the front of your mind, write it down if you have a journal, and remember it. In addition if you find something that you haven't been doing or avoiding, either consciously or unconsciously, after finding the answer and writing it down, keep it in mind. Your situation will not change unless you change it.

• On a personal note to you, take it from me, even if there are aspects you don't enjoy as much as others, if you face them head on and attack them full force you'll find, as your business develops, your job gets easier and easier and it isn't so painful to fix this anymore. My joint venture first contact for example is something I don't enjoy, but it's not necessary anymore, because people come to me. It had to be faced to get to this point though and I'd advise you to dig deep and do the same. It's quite likely you'll surprise yourself.

• Ok moving on again to something that I personally experienced and probably one of the biggest downfalls I've seen around me, in the past and no doubt in the future too, and that's getting attached to a product.

• The best example I can think of is when I had this old site going. Not a small site by any means. Anyway, I was constantly updating, cleaning, tidying, maintaining and so on. Meanwhile someone that I'd met just a few months earlier had pulled three sites out the bag, and these were serious sites, packed full of content.

• He said to me one day 'Hey, you've been working on that site a long time, it must be pretty huge by now'. It took me a while to realize why there were those of us that were moving forward and those of us not making a success of ourselves, and it was simple. Now there's nothing wrong with keeping customer support going and updating a site every now and then, especially if it's a membership site, but there are two important things to keep in mind. Firstly, don't get carried away changing, prettifying, adding, and so on. Secondly, don't try to be everything to everyone. If you already have happy customers, that's great. Your product is good, it's time to stop trying to fix it up and put that valuable time into creating multiple products and developing new ideas. It's the only way to move forward and learn.

• The moment I discovered this it set me free. Here I am now working on a serious amount of reports, sites, scripts, with a bigger list, better resources, more knowledge and experience under my belt, more promotion power, more contacts and strangely, more free time. If you want these things too, remember, never stop developing and moving forward. Keeping customer service up is one thing, but constantly going back and altering your ideas isn't the best way to do thing. Live and learn, and move on.

• Just to give you an idea of how powerful this alone is, here's a real life example. When I started out I met two different people. One already had their own site and one joined as a member of that site and was yet to create their own products. The one with the site is today, six or seven years later, working on that same site, still has a full time job and even though the site is massive and packed full of everything you could think of in their field of expertise, hasn't made much progress. The guy that joined this site as a member created sites, created content, products, learned, moved on, learned moved on, constantly pushed his boundaries. He told me yesterday that he has now quit his job and is earning on average $800 per day and moving towards doubling that within the year. This one aspect could be the difference between you failing, and your total success.

• Moving on to the next aspect of being worried you won't succeed. Many people seem to develop this over time, and have already made their mind up whether they're going to be a success or not.

• Now you may not be the type of person to worry about what other people are thinking or how they'll react to your products and the things you do, which is great, because you'll burn bridges a lot faster than us out there that hate it when someone doesn't like our work. This is why you'll always get the best from anything I do personally, but for those of you who are reading and get a little uptight when approaching something new this is for you.

• Let's get this all out in the open right now shall we? If you continue down this road you will on occasion experience the following. You will be shouted at, you will experience things that make you feel uncomfortable (namely change) you will be sworn at, you will be abused, called a liar, a money grabber, you will be refused, you will be denied, put down, told your work is shoddy, bad or not up to standard, and that the brand new idea you had won't ever work. No matter how good your work is this is inevitable whether it's from those that don't understand your work, a frustrated customer, someone who didn't like receiving an ad from you or someone who had their friend subscribe them to your stuff. Whatever it is, whether it was your fault or not, it will happen.

• Let's get something straight for one. You run your business the way you want to run it. It is your business, you're doing the work, creating the products, buying the guides, reaping the rewards. Don't ever, under any circumstances, let an abusive customer, negative friend, family member or frustrated customers that take their life out on you, either get you down or, put you off trying something new. Build new bridges, listen to people's advice along the way, but be confident, be determined, and physically hack and slash your way to success if you have to. This isn't desperation, this is sheer determination. Don't ignore advice, but flatten any obstacles in your way, gain new ground all day every day, and you'll find that it actually takes more effort for you not to make it than it does to make it.

• Finally, there's one more thing I'd like to get out in the open about being a success. That's doing everything on your own. Something that many marketers, that start their own business, like to do simply because it's such a change from their jobs, and they don't have anything else to worry about except customers. Either this or they think they'll be losing out on the profits side of things if they bring anyone else in on a deal. Totally the opposite is true.

• That's not to say that you need to go around partnering on every single site that you create, but it does mean that you need to think a little more about working in a team wherever possible.

• Partnerships are one example but you'll be splitting the profits 50/50. Lets say for example you both have the same amount of resources to get your promotion out to through different contacts and each others lists, affiliates, JV's and customers. Mix in a little bit of your expertise and you'll end up making the same amount of cash anyway if things are dead even. What you will get though is double the visitors, double the people in your follow-up, and double your affiliates adding fifty percent to your total income from the product to start with, and on top of that you'll be pulling in double the resources to promote to in the future.
• Don't worry if you don't have anyone on your contact list yet and you're starting from the very beginning, once you've launched your first few products you will have. Make it your business to work as a team. Make each other successful through plugging the gaps in your knowledge and ability with someone else and let them do the same in return. You will be more successful than you thought was possible with the product you work on, and due to increased resources, future products also.

• That's all for this section. Some of the smallest but yet the most important bits of information, all taken straight from real experiences we've had over here. Take the knowledge contained within this report, put it to good use, and I look forward to seeing many successful products come from you. Be careful though. Just because you don't have these problems right now, you may develop any of them later. Don't forget what you've just been reading and you'll do just fine.

Overview on Health

• To look at and put in place preventative measures to avoid physical discomfort or long term damage that can be done through the general wear and tear of everyday business online, and to look after your most important resource of all. You.

• To look at typing technique and how it can be quickly and habitually improved to avoid long term damage done to your hands, lower arms and wrists.

• To look at accessories that can help prevent long term damage to your hands, lower arms and wrists

• To look at techniques and habits that can be used to prevent disruption and degrading of your vision when sitting at a computer screen for long periods of time.

• To look at the comfort of your physical environment, and to avoid damage being done to your body through long periods of time spent in one sitting position.

• To take a look at what's around you, and how to use it to your advantage to stop yourself from becoming sick through over working and other health hazards.

• To look at basic psychological problems that may occur in the short term through the running of your day to day business, and how to avoid them, staying fresh, focused and stress free.

Staying Healthy

Important Note: We are not qualified doctors. These techniques have been developed through personal experience, and you should always go and see a physician or doctor before carrying any of them out, or if you're in doubt about your health and want further advice.

As online business owners ourselves we know all too well that negative effects can be brought upon ourselves through what we do. Sitting at computer screens, sometimes for long periods of time, sitting in the same position for long periods of time, making tens of thousands, even hundreds of thousands of key strokes per day can take its toll. Running your own business from day to day can take its toll when you're not prepared or not clued up on how to separate yourself from your workspace at the end of the day, all of which can quite easily lead to anything from bone problems, through to loss of sleep.

In this section, as strange as it may be for an online marketing report, we're going to look at a few of those causes, and what we do regularly to remove or negate the damage being done, and we're going to give you some of the techniques that we personally use so that you can put them to use for yourself.

This subject seems a little like taboo for some strange reason.

As an additional note before we get started, I have to point out that we are not qualified doctors, psychologists or physicians. What you're getting here is our personal experience. Before you try any of these consult a relevant and fully qualified authority on the matter.

Alright, let's get to it. What we're going to do is split this section up into small segments where we'll detail a problem, the long term effects, and what we do to make sure our bodies and minds don't go haywire and limit the damage done by each factor. I must stress, go and see someone qualified before using any of these as these methods may have different effects on different people.

Number One – The first thing I'd like to talk about is your hands, lower arms and wrists. We're sitting here typing all day for many days of the week. Constant pounding of the keys on the keyboard can get a little much for our health at times. If you're getting pains or twinges in your arms and wrists, either during or within twenty four hours of typing, it's a sign that we need to sort things out now, before they have a chance to get worse or to turn into an un-solvable problem.

(Wrist Support)
There are a couple of methods that I use personally to prevent this. The first of which is a set of light sports wrist supports. They're not splints, but have a very light and spongy texture. I don't wear them while I'm typing as they can restrict movement slightly and make the problem even worse, but I do wear them for a few hours afterwards. Due to their warming effect and promotion of circulation

within just a week of wearing them for an hour or so a day, stopped any little pains or twinges I was getting from writing the thousands of words every day for several months. Very handy and worth checking out. Make sure that your supports are not splinted and cover the whole wrist. In addition always buy a size bigger than you think you'll need. The way these things hug your arm, it's important they're not too tight, otherwise they may end up doing the opposite of what they're supposed to do. Similarly, don't do them up too tight either.

(Typing Position & Rests)
Next up is typing position and those rests that have become all the rage recently for both mouse and keyboard. Unfortunately most people use them incorrectly, possibly doing damage to their wrists and arms. If you actually check out the instructions and any reputable typing guide, or even the instructions that come with your rests, they should only be used when you're not typing. Using them while you're typing actually makes you stretch your wrists further, putting them under excess strain for sometimes long periods of time.

I want you to try an experiment right now. Go open yourself a new text document, and in your normal position, type out four or five lines, and pay attention to how that feels. Don't change anything at this point, just give it a shot and watch.

When you're done with that, open yourself a second document and write another few lines, but this time, lift your wrists and your hands off the keyboard and see how relaxed that feels compared to the other method. You'll also probably find that your arms get tired unless you raise your shoulders and sit up a little straighter instead of slouching, improving your posture at the same time. Give that a go now, see how it feels. It might be worth repeating this for a week or so in all your work until it becomes habit. As you can immediately feel, the strain on your wrists is dramatically reduced.

(Regular Breaks)
Next up, is something that everyone tells you to do, even your family and friends most likely if they see you at the computer for long periods of time, and that's to take regular breaks. When I say regular, I don't mean every four or five hours, which is so easy to do when you get wrapped up in a piece of work as I'm sure you've already noticed, but for a minute or so out of every twenty minutes. It's only three minutes an hour, but it's positive effects are definitely worth it. Increase this time if you want to, there's nothing stopping you doing this then taking an extra five minutes at the end of each hour. One thing I will say in addition to this, don't pull and prod, and stretch and curl your wrists when you take this break. It's supposed to take the pressure off and not be an extra workout. They get enough of that when they're put to work at your keyboard.

(Go see the doc)
Finally, if you have any doubts, need further information, or are having pains where there shouldn't be any, go and see a physician. It may seem like a lot of trouble over nothing, but what's the use in having a successful business if you're not in top health to enjoy it?

Number Two – Alright, second up we have any eyesight problems. There are several forms this can take, from short term blurry vision after long periods of staring at the screen, to excessive watering, or a burning sensation when you wake up in the morning and any form of dizziness. All signs which are at the very least annoyances, and at the very worst; problems that need to be sorted out early so you don't go on to do any long term damage.

(Regular Short Breaks)
The first thing that you need to do to prevent this happening, is of course, take regular breaks again! A minute every twenty, five minutes every hour, it's up to you. This is your business now. You don't have a boss telling you to stare at a screen twelve hours a day with only one or two breaks in between, even though you know that doing so isn't healthy. Find the right balance for yourself, and stick to it. While you're doing so, focus on something far away for a little while. I always find that if I've got real wrapped up in a bunch of work and stopped after many hours, there's kind of a partial short term short sightedness after all that staring. Not healthy. Focusing on something far away for a while helps get rid of it, but taking those regular breaks and preventing it altogether is a far better option.

(Go See Doc or optician)
Finally, if you have any long term problems, or a problem that exceed a particular point of severity, it's time to go and see an optician or someone qualified to fix you up.

Number Three, we have back pains or stiffness, especially in the lower back or shoulders. It's possible that this could quite easily be your posture and your general comfort when you're sitting at your workplace. A great example of this is when I moved into this place. When I walked in all there was to sit on was a wooden chair. Eager to get on with this business, before anything else was unpacked, or any new furniture was bought, I spent a day, maybe a day and half sat on this chair. I'll tell you, my back hurt for days afterwards, and I was glad to get back to normal. So if you're sitting on an uncomfortable chair that makes you feel like you slept in a strange position, it might be time to make an investment in a large, reclining office chair, with cushioned seats and a high back. They don't cost a lot nowadays and are well worth the investment.

Add to this a good lot of walking around during your break, a good posture, helped by the position we talked about previously when we discussed typing technique, and you have a great combination for many comfortable working days.

Number Four, now here's a little something that I had to deal with myself, coming literally straight out of a standard nine to five job, turning my efforts to working at home, spending many hours at the computer trying to figure out all of these marketing techniques you see before you. Making that switch isn't as easy at seems. My friends used to say to me, hey you're lucky. You earn more money than I probably ever will in the jobs that I go for, you get to work whenever you like for however long you like, and do whatever you want whenever you want to do it. Of course until they've experienced this for themselves, they don't realize it's not quite that easy. Even business owners who use an office can come home at the end of the day and forget about their work but us as online marketers are different.

The computer and your work is always right there, right in front of you. It's all to easy to walk past the computer and find out an hour later that you've just been going through business ideas in your head instead of enjoying that time out that you planned. It can effect concentration and sleep, especially if your computer and business tools are in a prominent place in your house. So here's the thing. To help you disconnect at the end of the day, get that computer right out of your bedroom and your sleeping area if it's there. If you have a spare bedroom, why not make it into an office if you haven't done so already? It might allow you to get your computer and work stuff out of your main living quarters, so that when you go to relax, you really are relaxing and leaving it behind at the end of the day.

The method of tying up loose ends and disconnecting is one that really helped before I was able to remove my work from my main living quarters, hence the reasons we've been doing that since the start of the course in a really habit forming way through repetition.

Number Five, here's a little something shocking I found out just over eight months ago. Did you know that the average office space contains thirty times more bacteria than the average toilet seat? That's pretty manky, but I can see how it happens. Grabbing some food, or a drink after working, going out for a quick smoke, a couple of drinks around the place, a few computer upgrades here and there. You know how it is. I know personally my computer desk sees pretty much every part of my life, and because of that, it gets a good solid anti-bac every night after I'm done with it. For general health reasons, it might be good to just chuck an anti bac spray can or a pack of wipes so you can quickly mop up ready for the next morning, including your mouse and keyboard especially. Cans of compressed air for your keyboard are also a must. You can get these from many reputable office supply stores.

Number Six, moving to leg pains. Something that can come about for a number of reasons. The ones I'm getting at right now are due to poor circulation. A numb foot, calf pains and spasms could well be related to your seating arrangements. Another good reason for you to head out and buy a really good chair for yourself with good soft cushioning behind the knees. It really is a top priority if we're going to keep you comfortable and everything in good working order.

In addition to this, get up and go for a walk every time you take one of your breaks. Meanwhile you can be grabbing a drink, focusing on something further away to re-align your eyes if needs be. It really is beneficial. I gotta say as well, that this is pretty hard to do. I'm used to talking about online marketing and business, not what you on a daily basis and how you live your life, so if I sound like I'm doing anything here but relaying information to you from my research as an online marketer, than I apologize. That's all this is, a little bit of handy info to keep you in top condition, leaving your mind free to make your business a success.

That's it. That's all there is to it. There's not going to be a summary section for healthy online marketing, because we're all as bullet pointed up as we can go with this.

Number seven, and finally, any other health worries or problems you may have. Go see a doc, physician, psychologist, whoever can help you. Solving problems is a big part of business, so is preventing damage by putting precautionary measures in place. Are yours in place, or are you doing yourself damage as we speak? A healthy business owner equals a healthy business.

Acton Points
• To re-cover and re-iterate some of the most important points put forward to you throughout the course, namely the biggest reasons you'll be successful, and the biggest reasons that may stop you from achieving your goals, and talk about how to take advantage of them.

• To discuss the right frame of mind for business success, and show you how to use this information to emulate the successful, and ultimately get there yourself in the shortest period of time possible.

• To re-iterate the importance of staying healthy. A healthy business owner means a far greater chance of a healthy business.

• To re-visit the habit forming exercise of taking your fifteen minutes out after each days work, to show you now what you've achieved by doing so throughout the course, where others who didn't will have likely failed.

• To talk further about the development of your business, the time it's going to take, and the positive signs that you'll be seeing, and should have already begun to experience that show you that you're heading in the right direction.

• To introduce other aspects of online marketing that may prove helpful for further learning in the future, and to show you that the way we've done things is one of many methods that actually work.

• To persuade you to dive in head-first every day.

Monitoring Your Success
At all times I want you to be looking at yourself and your business. Are you moving forwards? What have you achieved in the passed 48 hours working on your business? If you're looking at the same page on your screen, with the same content then it's time to start asking questions and looking for the problem.

I'm not saying you have to be super-efficient all the time, we all have good days and bad days, where we'll inevitably get more or less done that we know we should, but there's this little problem of moving onwards and upwards that many people can't seem to grasp. If you're reading this, you've already proved that you have grasped this concept, now as straight forward as it sounds, it's amazing to see how people do one of three things.

Factors That Hinder Success

The first is they either jump from guide to guide taking in the knowledge but not doing anything about it, and never moving forward. This was me several years ago, until I realized I actually had all this knowledge and knew in depth and often more about a subject than the actual author. It was time to start asking questions. Turns out I had all the knowledge already, but just didn't know it. Are you in the same position? Is it time to stop reading and start acting on the knowledge that you've gained?

Second is the broken the vase syndrome related to being pro-active or reactive. Imagine you wake up in the morning and decide you're going to clean the house up that day. You jump out of bed, jump in the shower have breakfast, and wash the dishes afterwards, the clean the surfaces. You've improved the kitchen already by cleaning the surfaces and doing the dishes right? Not so, you've just been reactive, and carried out required maintenance and things are now back to how they were when you first woke up. No progress, just reactive maintenance.

So you head out to the hall ready to do some dusting, and on the way out you break a vase, so out comes the Hoover, and you Hoover up all the bits and take the broken bits outside, and make everything nice and clean again. After putting your stuff away, you realize you cut your leg on a sharp plant outside. No matter, you head upstairs, give it a clean and place a plaster on it, then head back downstairs. What have you achieved so far? Nothing at all. This is reactive maintenance also, because there's no progress, you're literally just maintaining. It's important to distinguish between proactive and reactive, because quite often you can come home after a hard days work and you might be so tired and feel like you got a lot done and moved forward, when actually all you did was pull out a bit of maintenance.

It's the same with business. If you sit down at your computer and do your maintenance, answer some mails, change the color of your site, talk to a few people about what's been going on, have a look at a few products, there's nothing here to move you forward. Create those products, develop those products, enhance those ideas, write those sales letters, contact those JV's, gain knowledge and understanding and get real tired doing it and I guarantee you'll be moving forward at such a fast pace no one will know how you're doing it. Whilst they're tired and say things like "Wow I'm real tired and I still haven't got much done" now you know why, and how to avoid it. Of course maintenance is a big part of every day life and needs to be done, but learn to differentiate between the two, learn to spot them and recognize them and you'll immediately see a difference in your speed and efficiency. Give it a go, and you won't be disappointed.

This brings me on to the final type of person that doesn't succeed. The maintainer. The prettying up the website twelve times a year, the adding bundles and bundles of stuff to a membership site and their current market instead of creating new products and breaking into new markets and creating multiple specialized income streams. Think about that next time you go to redesign something. Are you redesigning because your tracking tells you that your redesign will make more sales, pull more leads or more resources? Or are you doing it because it doesn't quite look as nice as you'd like. Don't get stuck in the circle of ever improving without moving on, because you might just find yourself in the same place in a year's time, just with a slightly prettier website. Not proactive, productive or profitable at all. I know many people who have fallen into this trap, and in fact some people still in that trap and aren't looking like they'll be getting out of it very soon. Avoid it at all costs and you'll do fine, move forward, move forward quickly, and gain valuable knowledge and first hand experience along the way, something no one can put a price on because It's just that valuable.

These aspects are more important than most will ever discover for themselves, and if you remember back to the top ten reasons for success section, the above was put in there too, simply because I can't help but push this and push this because it really is the difference between getting somewhere and not getting anywhere at all. There's no in between. This should be your top priority, more important than that product creation, more important than making any sales, more important than resource building or any marketing method anyone can ever teach you.

Next up, let's look at your frame of mind. I honestly believe through personal experience that being in the right frame of mind to get your business moving onwards and upwards quickly is again, more important than any marketing tactic that you can learn.

The best way without a doubt is to end your day with 15 minutes of quiet thought. It's like keeping a journal, and helps you not only prepare for the day ahead, but sort out any problems you may have stumbled upon without the need to get stressed about it. In addition, it'll give you a clear picture of exactly where to go next. Practice this often and within a few days, you'll start to see some positive and quite strange results.

Always look forward, and take that time out to look inwards from that window (That's you looking at yourself from outside a window to gain a better perspective on what's going on in your business) It's real important for your development and the development of your business. If you haven't experienced this yet, it's all about evaluating your situation and your business with an open mind. Like dreaming, sleeping, it assists the organization of your thoughts. You'll begin to see problems and present solutions to them before they even happen. Hindsight is a very powerful thing, and taking this important time out on a daily basis allows you to prepare for future situations that may arise, which is partially hindsight, but more crystal clear, focused and pure thinking at it's best. I haven't met anyone that's not capable of this yet, so if you're unsure, give it a shot and watch what begins to happen six or seven sessions, and I assure you, you won't be disappointed.

As important as the above is the way in which you end your day when you're working. Remember to disconnect, and I don't mean just from the Internet, I mean totally. This method of pulling off the relaxing and reflection, looking from the outside in then after you're done, whether it's ten minutes, or thirty minutes later, you turn your computer off for the night. You leave your place of work, turn it off, and forget about everything. Keeping your distance from your work isn't something that's easy to do, especially if you have your computer in your bedroom. Even working at home and walking past it ten times a day is enough to spark thoughts, which will take your mind off your daily life and some of your important daily tasks, and sometimes even disrupt sleep. This is definitely something we want to avoid.

Let me ask you this, have you ever been called by your husband or wife, or family member for something? Anything at all, either, dinner is ready! Or ok, I'm ready to go out now, are we going? Or even more likely, I'm off to bed now, are you coming too? And your reply comes something like this. 'Hold on! I'll be there in a moment, I just need to do this first'.

Another example of this type of mindset going full steam ahead is coupled with the above examples, you have to keep getting out of bed at night, or keep walking out the door ready to go, starting the car and going back to the computer because you forgot to do something, or you have to do something before you go. Classic one that.

This is why it's important to do both of these exercises. Observe your self, and your business, relax, look from the outside in, then when you're done, cut it off. Disconnect, turn your computer off safe in knowledge you haven't forgotten anything, you don't need to worry about anything and you don't need to wake up in the middle of the night and spend hours doing something that you planned to only take a few minutes. Trust me on this one, I'm not giving you instructions or how to run your life, far from it, but be careful not to get too involved all of the time or that freedom and easy life progress you've made so far might just evaporate. There's speed, efficiency and determination, but then there's another level of speed efficiency and determination. Just because you're not working on your business longer than your body or mind can comfortably handle, doesn't mean that you're slacking.

Next up comes a little something I've been a fan of since without noticing it, I managed to develop random back pains, wrist pains and aching, and short sightedness in my left eye and gain some four stone in weight (which is all gone now finally).

Stay healthy. Above all, above everything taught in this guide stay healthy. Take note of the keeping healthy section of the course. Get a good chair, look after your back. Get some of those wrist supports one size bigger than you need, type correctly, look after your wrists, and look after your eyes and belly. Take regular breaks and pull regular exercise, even if it means you go out and buy some weights and run a little everyday.

Again, I'm not trying to tell you how to live your life by any means, but it's important to me that if you're going to be a success in the future, you come to me and say 'Your report spurred me into action and I'm now pulling in every month what I earned in my last job every year' and not 'Your report spurred me into action and I'm now pulling in every month what I earned in my last job every year, but I gained a hundred pounds, developed carpal tunnel syndrome, my back hurts and I can't see much anymore'. No way, not on my watch. Health is always number one. It's no good being successful if you're too sick to enjoy it.

Prepare Yourself

We already talked about how things don't always go to plan, when launching new sites, when creating ad campaigns, contacting people, creating joint ventures, whatever it might be, it's possible it may go pear shaped. Thankfully, this is rare, but prepare yourself, because if it does happen you'll need patience, you'll need determination and a clear and sharp mind to sort out problems quickly.

If you find yourself awake at 5am wondering why you didn't go to bed when you decided (five hours ago), don't fret you're not alone. In fact, as I write this report it's 6.20am, almost 24 hours after I started writing, and I'm still here because the previous texts didn't quite live up to the standard I'd planned, and with the launch date drawing closer, it needs to be done. Don't do this intentionally mind, and don't make a habit of it, because it be very damaging to a lot of things including your health, but when things don't work out as planned, prepare to have to put more in than you originally planned to.

In addition if you find yourself awake at ridiculous times and you find you're making a lot of mistakes and it's just been a heck of a long day, disconnect, turn off and walk away and continue tomorrow. There's only a need to do this on the odd occasion that something goes wrong with a site launch. Everything else can wait.

Ideas for Your Business

Keep your imagination and mind working at all times. Once you launch your first product if you haven't already you will immediately begin to see that ideas begin to come automatically. Unless you mix with your market, it's very hard to come up with ideas to solve problems when you don't know what the problem is in the first place.

Mix with your market. This is something that we all need to be doing on at least a weekly basis, watching other people, watching their products and their marketing methods, watching as their mailings come to you, and looking at their techniques, their copy, their products and so on. This isn't for any reasons related to copying, we already talked about emulation and how to carry this out correctly, taking someone else's methods and plugging them into your products without copying any aspect from them at all. The reason for this is solely to keep your mind awake and to keep it producing idea after idea after idea.

Here's an example of how this works. In the last week, whilst actively taking an interest in other marketers and what they're doing, listening in to their lists as a research tool as we already discussed earlier, I've come up with no less than fifteen viable ideas for products and double that number for methods of presentation. Some wild and some wacky, but they are ideas all the same.

This is why it's easier to pull ideas once you've launched your own product and began to watch other marketers and ask why they're doing what they're doing. You're mixing with new marketing methods, creating a basis for your tracking and new ideas, and you're experiencing the market first hand, allowing you to come up against, discover and ultimately solve problems with your products through this research, your experience, the scripts and services you use to promote your products, and the guides you read. They're all important to you in this way because they will form the basis of your ideas. If you're not mixing with your market you won't know any of the problems, and won't be able to solve them, and thus won't have any product ideas.

As an additional note to this, those fifteen ideas I came up with is a weekly occurrence because I've been doing this since 1999. Don't worry if you don't reach that figure, don't strain to reach it. Just one of your ideas may turn out to be more profitable than all my fifteen put together. By the time you've launched two or three products, using the methods In this guide you'll likely find that you don't have enough time in the world to bring all your ideas to life; you'll be having too many of them. So there we have it. Mix with your market. It will keep your creative juices flowing, form the basis of new knowledge and experiences and go down as one of the most important aspects of your online marketing and idea creation processes.

Making Progress

Ok, moving on again, I should let you know that things are gradual. No overnight millionaire mindset here. I'm not saying for a moment that it's slow, you can find yourself with a list of ten thousand plus from a single product, even when starting out, a good bunch of contacts and a load of affiliates.

Whilst moving forward it may help you to keep this in mind. 'Keep your business a real business'. Keep creating real products and selling sheer quality to real people and you will move forward. Don't get wrapped up the craze and the dreams of millions in days. Have dreams sure, but I don't want anyone to wake up one morning and find themselves misguided by some cowboy, or the focus taken away from their business by some sort of earnings scheme that offers them something for nothing, or a lot too quickly. You know the claims, the ones where it's almost too good to be true. No doubt you've heard this before, if it seems too good to be true, it probably is. Don't lose that real business frame of mind, and remember what we're about in this game. This will allow you to protect yourself, your pocket, achieve focus and keep moving towards your goals and that of your business without distractions and the minimum of mistakes along the way. If you can make sure that you're moving forward and can see progress every time you leave your workstation, you're well on the way and have won half the battle.

- The Key to Quick Success

Next up, keep building those resources, every chance you get. Every JV you pull, every ad you send, every person you contact, every person that contacts you, subscribes to your list, or whatever. Start to think in terms of resources instead of sales because these are the key to your success, the resources not the sales. Of course the resources are there to make you sales, but without them there's little profit in online marketing no matter how good you might be at promotion.

This brings me back to the previous point about gradual growth. It's important that you do not underestimate what you have at your disposal. Just a small number of the quality resources that we already talked about can be extremely profitable. A single JV can span multiple products and several years for example. Just a single JV. A single affiliate can pull in thousands of resources, just five thousand quality subscribers can be responsible for thousands per month, and that's even before we look at joint ventures and affiliates. So you see, just because you have to build resources, and I keep telling you that it won't be instant, I wouldn't be surprised if most people are thinking a year or two to get to where they want to be. Of course, it is gradual, business in general as well as with your resource building, but depending on the deals you pull and how quickly and effectively you can make the progress using your knowledge, it's not the several years job you might be feeling a little anxious about.

An additional note to that, always keep your resources building each other. Taking each resource, separating them into categories, and using each one to build another often allows you to pull many times the profit from a single set of resources that you may have previously kept separate and only profited once from them.

Also remember what this does in terms of you vs. every other online marketer out there. While they're out there paying for ads over and over and saying things like 'This online marketing game is a scam I can never make any profit' or something to that effect for many years. This is simply because they keep spending their money on stuff again and again and not pulling anything from it but a few sales. Using the methods you've learned here, build, and multiply, and let things snowball, and before you know it, you won't actually be cornered into spending money on your promotion like all the rest that don't understand this resource building and multiplication technique.

Mistakes Are Good

Next up, my fave. Make lots of mistakes. We like mistakes, because they teach us something every time we make them. If you're not making any mistakes, it's time to look at the way in which you're working. Are you sticking to the stuff that you know best, and avoiding breaking new ground because you're worried about making mistakes?

This course is here to minimize the mistakes made when using these methods, but that doesn't mean you won't make any at all. All of this information is in our heads, yet we still make mistakes. Every time we make one and find the solution, that's another tool, another ally we can add to our arsenal that we didn't have before. Make mistakes, screw up every now and then and learn something new, but be groundbreaking, be pioneering, be imaginative and be confident.

In addition to the previous point, have you made a mistake? Excellent, learn from it but don't let it hold you back from trying something new or going down that road again once you've gained more knowledge and experience.

I Can't, Because...

Finally, but equally as important as all that we've discussed so far, have you ever spoken to someone who really wants to do something, whether it's set up a business, or travel somewhere, or do something that they don't necessarily do every day and when you've asked them why they don't do it, they say 'I would, but..' Often that but is followed by something like 'I don't know how' or 'I'll probably mess it up' or 'I don't know if it will work'. These a prime examples of condemning a project or an attempt at a project to failure before it's even been tried and prevents that all important forward movement.

If you can say for a fact, something won't work through research and tracking, that's fine, that's common sense and logical deduction using facts, but don't scare monger or condition yourself to be worried about biting the bullet and going for it. After all, what is there to stop you aside from worries about something not working? In actuality, this isn't anything that's stopping you, because you're the one who controls your own mind. It's totally up to you.

Take the plunge. Never say I can't. Most of the time when people say they can't, they can, but they either have to face a fear or give something up to get what they want. Go for it. What is stopping you launching your own products using the techniques here? Is there any real reason that makes it not possible to move forward at this point?

All the best with your business!

Action Points

• First, whole idea of this report, its goals, its summaries and write-ups was to get you moving forward with your business.

• Whatever was stopping you previously from achieving success should now be eliminated and through the methods you've been taught, you will immediately be able to see if you're moving forward or not moving at all with your business.

• Keep it moving forward at a pace. Don't get bogged down, watch yourself closely. Are you being proactive or Reactive? Have you progressed in the last 48 hours? If you're staring at the same things you had two days ago, it's time to start asking questions.

• Remember what we talked about when looking at reasons for success, these are the most important things to keep in mind, even over product creation, actual marketing techniques or anything like that.

• You have to be in the right frame of mind to succeed, those relaxation techniques, quiet time to evaluate the situation, looking from the outside to in. Keep doing them and you will start to see an extreme rate of development in your business.

• Once you're done working for the night, carry out the exercises then disconnect and walk away. In addition health wise, keeping yourself up at night worrying about your business won't do you and productive favours.

• Stay healthy. I don't want anyone reading this to go off on a psycho one, developing a bunch of products and getting rich if they're going to destroy their health doing it. It's no good being sick and successful.

• Prepare yourself. Sheer dogged determination is sometimes needed when the hours get long, and things don't always go as you planned them.

• Keep your imagination and mind working at all times. Once you launch your first product if you haven't already you will immediately begin to see that ideas begin to come automatically. Unless you mix with your market, it's very hard to come up with ideas to solve problems when you don't know what the problem is in the first place.

• Things are gradual. Don't expect to wake up rich one morning, we all know it doesn't work like that in real business, again, keep moving forward, and if you can see development and forward movement each and every week, you've won half the battle.

• Keep building those resources. Every chance you get, these are the key to your success. Building all five at the same time is easy when you begin launching your own products. Wielding even a small number of affiliates, customers, JVs, long-term customers and lists hold immense power in so many situations.

• Keep your resources building each other. It's important that they are all built together and managed correctly at all times. Keep this in mind and you'll have an almost unlimited number of resources and little trouble snowballing this at a faster and faster pace the more products you launch.

• Make lots of mistakes. This course is here to minimize this, but as with going to school or learning any new skill, without practicing it literally, it's hard to get good. Making mistakes is good. Every single 'do this' and 'don't do that' piece of advice in this course has been pulled from mistakes as well as successes.

• Made a mistake? Great, learn from it, and move on. Don't let it hold you back or scare monger you into never trying anything new or trying again when you have more experience. Similarly, don't let anyone scare you off. The internet is full of all sorts of people, some will inevitably take a frustrating day out on you through the business.

• Take the plunge. Never say I can't. Most of the time when people say they can't, they can, but they either have to face a fear or give something up to get what they want. Go for it. What is stopping you launching your own products using the techniques here? Is there any real reason that makes it not possible to move forward at this point?

Success To You, You Now Own It!